Helping BOYS Learn

6 Secrets for your son's success in school

Parent Edition

by Dr. Edmond J. Dixon

www.helpingboyslearn.com

Copyright © 2013 Edmond J. Dixon

ISBN-13: 978-1492171713
ISBN-10: 1492171719

Table of Contents

ACKNOWLEDGEMENTS

There are a number of people who helped me to complete the parent edition of this book. Christina Luce, has provided invaluable insights into how this approach can be used with boys. Sandy Bergquist, Amy Hunter, Marion Raymundo, Joanne Kapsos, Tracey Lorusso, Mari Kingshot, and Kathleen Does-Koehl reviewed the book prior to publication and helped me improve and refine it. Emilie Shumway and Catherine Fish were my excellent copyeditors. Kendra Grant supplied icons for the six secrets. Heather Down at Wintertickle Press took on the book layout and design and provided me with important advice during the publication process.

There were also those not involved with the actual writing who made it possible for me to do this work. First of all, there were the countless parents, teachers, and students with whom I worked over the past few years. They helped me develop this approach to boys' learning and will be responsible for helping many more benefit from it. In terms of organization, Dennis Croft has been an invaluable advisor, giving me encouragement and guidance that has made it possible for me to launch the *Helping Boys Learn* initiative throughout North America. And finally, my wife Joanne, whose support over these many years and wisdom in raising our own sons has taught me much and allowed me to pursue this mission to help every boy learn and reach his potential.

NOTE ABOUT REFERENCES

This book is based on both my experience working with boys for more than 30 years and recent research on brain development and boys. To make it easier on the reader I have chosen not to interrupt the flow of the book with references and notes. When I have used ideas from a specific source, however, I point that out and it will be easy for you to find more information on the internet. A short list for further reading can be found at the end of the book and I can provide more detailed references via email at dr.dixon@helpingboyslearn.com.

FOREWORD

This book is for those who want to help the boys in their lives be successful. *Helping Boys Learn* will give you what you need to help that young man love learning and perform better at home, in school, and throughout life. Although this book is addressed to parents, it is also for you if you are a guardian, grandparent, aunt, or uncle—or just a friend to a boy. If you have known this boy for any length of time you are well prepared for this! You have already been a teacher to him in your various interactions, whether you realized it or not. You may have also used some of the "6 Secrets" with him, albeit unconsciously. Now you will gain a better understanding of how these secrets powerfully sync with the male brain's natural learning preferences and how they can motivate a boy to unleash the tremendous potential he possesses.

Empowering a boy to tap into his own reserves of understanding, commitment and resilience is the key to life-long success and is what our education system is supposed to do. Lately, however, schools have had trouble fulfilling this mission for millions of boys. As a result, not only do many boys fail in school, but they fail to see themselves as learners in any context, cutting themselves off from the opportunity for better, more productive, and happier lives. Their failure to reach their potential affects not only their lives, but those of their families and friends as well as the very fabric of our communities.

It is because successful learning is so important that home and school need to be intertwined. With the right approach, success in one area can foster success in the other. But it is best done consciously, with attention to what actually helps boys learn. That is what this book will provide. It is based on the most recent brain research and my own 30-plus years of experience as a teacher, principal, researcher—and parent of boys. It is written in easy-to-understand language and designed to provide you with tools that can help a boy learn more successfully at home and at school.

By reading this, you show your commitment to helping your son become a happy and successful learner. Perhaps he has not been successful in school; perhaps he was an enthusiastic learner before going to school, but is resistant to classroom learning. Maybe, when you hear from his teacher, it is about how he is having problems and is unable to focus. Possibly he has been identified as having "special needs" or has been recommended for testing and/or medication. These are all stressful situations for children and parents and you may wonder how you can help him to be the kid you know he can be. I am here to tell you that—no matter what the situation in school—you can have a profound and positive effect on that boy's learning.

The first step is to create understanding based on the right kind of information. So what "secrets" can this book provide? A look at the table of contents reveals familiar words like *movement, game,* and *challenge.* How can these things be secrets? I like to compare it to a game my family played as during long car trips. Our parents would challenge us to try to spot the red model of the Volkswagen Beetle and keep tally of how many we saw. As we started to play the game, we saw many we had never noticed before. Even in the weeks following the game, the car seemed to be *everywhere* and we wondered why there were so many on the road lately. Of course, there were no more Beetles on the road than before, but now we were aware of them. The cars were the same, but we were different. Anaïs Nin wrote, "We do not see the world as it is, we see it as we are."

Your view of the world of boys' learning will be different when you see it through the lens of these six pathways and discover the untapped power they offer parents to influence their son's learning. My own experience has convinced me that these secrets are important to all boys, but particularly important for boys who struggle in school. You, too, can use these six pathways to take what you already know and experience with these boys (or more correctly, their male brains) and put them to use daily. It will provide you with both "aha!" moments and concrete, definable ways to foster engagement, achievement, independent growth, and success with boys.

The practical application of what you learn here cannot be stressed enough. You will be given powerful knowledge and be encouraged to use it. A process will be provided to help you use what you learn with your son, and you will be supported by a range of online resources designed to help him grow stronger as a learner. This support means that this book is not an end in itself, but the beginning of a journey that will bring learning, joy, and success to everyone involved.

INTRODUCTION
What's Up With Boys in School?

"Of all the animals, the boy is the most unmanageable."
—Plato

It's in the air: concern about boys and school. In the past 10 years, an ever-increasing amount of educational literature in North America has been devoted to disengaged, low-achieving, dropping-out young males. An overview of the research indicates that girls outperform boys at every grade level. Boys make up more than 65% of the students in special education, are much more likely to be diagnosed with autism and attention deficit disorders, are more likely to be held back a grade, and are twice as likely to drop out of school. The problem is particularly acute in areas of poverty.

It is easy to test the findings of the research at the ground level. Ask any teacher you know to think about students who struggle most in class. Then ask how many of those students are male—I am confident you will discover that 75% of them are boys. It wasn't long ago when we were vitally concerned with the problem of girls learning in school. What happened to that problem? Did we solve it so well that we disadvantaged boys in the process? And what about the glass ceiling? Doesn't it still exist? Isn't it still a pretty good world for the boys?

The unease about boys and learning right now is well placed. Indeed, their perceived problems may be much greater in the future than we realize. The policies to help girls in school have had a strongly positive impact over the past 20 years. Yet the world has changed tremendously due to the Internet and our worldwide connectivity. Girls' natural brain wiring ideally suits them to the challenges of an information-filled, collaborative, and post-modern society and places them in a learning sweet spot for our age. Supported by the policies that were put in place to help them succeed at school in the 1990s, they are more successful in school at every level. We will see females progressively mirroring this success in the 21st century workplace, breaking any and all barriers left in the glass ceiling. This is an obvious benefit to them and to society.

On the other hand, the fact that many boys fall behind in school and fail to complete education at the higher levels required for effective future employment means they will be increasingly at a disadvantage to participate meaningfully. If history is any indicator, large numbers of unemployable and increasingly angry and frustrated young men are not good for any society. It can result, for one, in a violent and crime-ridden environment; it can also result in a culture of impoverished entitlement where men "play" all the time, but make little contribution—all the while being supported financially and emotionally by others. To a certain extent, evidence of this latter path is already appearing. Hanna Rosin's *The End of Men* is one book in a whole spate of what I would call "males are not fitting in" literature that is mirrored by their snowballing disengagement in school.

In reality, both genders need to succeed equally in our educational systems for our social well-being. Addressing the challenges that boys face in school doesn't mean that girls will be disadvantaged. Indeed, finding true equity means recognizing what each child needs to learn. And for you, as a parent, it is crucial: What does my son need to learn best?

We know from neuroscience that the real learning happens when people are engaged and motivated to learn. How can we motivate boys to learn? I am convinced the answer lies in channeling the strong tendencies that boys have developed through thousands of years to help them learn and survive in the world. When we create environments that do that, boys' learning becomes easier. They develop the confidence and skills to use their talents effectively side by side with girls in ways that are positive for everyone. In school, it is important that boys see the classroom as a place where he can learn.

Why is the classroom so important? Because despite the tremendous benefits a school can provide to boys in terms of athletics, social opportunities, and technological support, success in the traditional classroom environment has been the clearest indicator of success in both higher education and the broader society for the vast majority of men during past 50 years. Likewise, consistent failure in the classroom is the surest predictor of disengagement from school, disciplinary problems, dropping out, unemployment, drug use, and criminality in males. This makes sense because education has always been a great equalizer, a pathway to help those from any economic or social background find greater success and contribute to society.

As I argued in *KEEN for Learning*, despite the fact that the classroom is an artificial environment in which we suspend the normal activities of life, we rely heavily on this environment to help students learn. That may be changing with increasing online education, but it is still the way society expects children to learn in school. One of the reasons people still go to school for classroom learning, despite the new learning opportunities available to individuals through the media and the Internet, is that most adults were taught in classrooms when they were young. It is so familiar that each of us feels that, in a sense, we understand the classroom. But for many boys, especially those who struggle, the classroom is an alien environment that appears set up for one express purpose: *to keep them from learning.* A 6-year-old boy may not express this in words, but he knows it—feels it—intuitively. Some of you reading this will have a son who loves to learn, yet hates school.

The Fear Factor

When learning does not involve the six secrets I highlight in this book, a significant number of boys try and fail time after time in the classroom environment. Remember the Peanuts cartoon in which Lucy pulls the football away every time Charlie Brown tries to kick it? Charlie wants to be successful; however, each time he tries, the ball is pulled away and he lands flat on his back. I have seen it repeated over and over in school: boys who want to believe that they can learn, but who, despite their best efforts, experience difficulties over and over again. Even worse, Charlie Brown has at least an inkling that it's Lucy's fault he's missing the ball, but a seven-year-old boy can't fathom that his parents or teachers would ever do such a thing. So he internalizes it. He begins to believe that he's the problem, he's defective, he's the failure. As we'll see, his brain has been wired by evolution in such a way that he must survive in a threatening environment. He will therefore increasingly exhibit "fight or flight" reactions, which can continue predictably for many years—until he can free himself of formal education and its constraints. But we know that such "freedom" actually imprisons an uneducated boy with the bondage of unfulfilled expectations, limited life choices, and self-loathing. Do you think I exaggerate? I have talked with too many heartbroken parents who now despair for their sons, who grew into young adults saddled with the belief that they could not learn. This affects those young men profoundly, and is often reflected in self-destructive actions or refusal to pursue any positive pathways that might require a school-like environment.

We know from research that learning is the result of neural pathways in the brain. We also know that the brain creates those pathways by paying attention to the experiences each of us have—in school and out. But it does not pay the same degree of attention to every experience. There are too many things going on around us. In his book, The Mind's Past, neuroscientist Michael Gazzinga estimates that 99% of the sensory data that comes into our brains is discarded. That is why you can sit at a city café near traffic and after a while not really "hear" it anymore. You can hear it in reality, but your brain has decided it's not important enough to pay attention to on a conscious level. If we didn't have this filtering ability, we would never really free our minds to focus on anything, and we most likely would never have grown into the complex learners that we are. But the filtering system is very sensitive: If you were in the café and heard a loud screeching sound, you would immediately direct your attention toward it. This is because the brain's primitive warning mechanisms are kicking in to keep you safe, telling you to direct your attention toward something that might threaten your safety. In other words, the traffic sounds now mean something to you. But this meaning is based on fear.

Fear is a good way to create neural pathways that keep you safe in the jungle or in traffic, but it is not effective in school—particularly in our modern world. In boys in particular, it is processed in the primitive parts of the brain, including the amygdala, which evolved to prepare our bodies for fight-or-flight danger. This region is larger in boys and causes fearful emotions that shut down the frontal lobes, the exact parts of the brain needed for success in learning. This reversion to the ancient fight-or-flight approach happens often when boys face what they perceive as overwhelming odds. In other words, when they feel that "they can't win." Because fear causes such stress on the body, it can't be maintained and is ineffective in motivating a long-term commitment to learning. Likewise, because fear is based on losing something, it focuses the mind on the immediate task of avoiding the loss and not the deeper understanding. Fear was a motivator for some learning in the past when if you didn't learn a skill (spear throwing) you might not eat, but the same threat is not present when learning fractions.

A brain-friendly way for boys to learn

I have made a concentrated effort in this book to avoid jargon and complex terms, but there are two new concepts that you need to understand if you want to use the 6 secrets to the best effect with boys. The first is *motivated engagement*. While fear will not create the neural connections in the brain necessary for school success, motivated engagement supercharges learning because it uses joy to connect us with learning. Recall the smile on your boy's face when he first learned to walk or discovered something new in the grass. Look at the gleam in his eyes when he scores a goal, plays a video game, listens to music he loves, or watches a favorite television program. That happiness comes from learning! It is the joy of growth and all humans crave it. It causes us to look toward the future, dream dreams, and imagine what could be. This type of learning feeds growth and pulls us toward our own potential.

It also brings forth a second phenomenon. *Discretionary effort* is used when we do things that we are not required to do. It's demonstrated when we work that extra bit, go that extra mile, or connect a part of our identity with what we are doing and, by doing so, make it our own. It places us within an activity, actively seeking to influence it. It's something we do, not something done to us. It leverages the creation of neural pathways in the frontal lobes and brings our creativity to any problem—and it supercharges learning! But as its name implies, it is controlled completely by the individual. It is easily withheld, even when it looks like someone is giving their best. It cannot be demanded or required—only invited. The most pervasive social media phenomenon of our era is totally built on discretionary effort. Facebook is an online platform which has minimal features and structure and has no meaning until we use our discretionary effort to fill it up with information about ourselves and our world. And why do we do it? Because we have *motivated engagement* with the joy that comes from sharing ourselves with others. It's very simple, really. But it's the secret to Facebook's phenomenal success. In the same way, if you use the ideas provided in this book, you can pave the way for a boy's success in school.

Boys and Girls Learn Differently

My approach proceeds from the belief that boys are hard-wired to learn in certain ways. Not all boys are hard-wired in the exact same way, but when you put groups of boys together the way we do in school, it is a great predictor of their approach to learning. Those of us who have worked with boys and girls for long periods of time see this clearly, and there is also a great deal of research supporting this view.

Anyone who observes children sees the difference this hardwiring produces. The description that follows is something I actually observed in a local café; any parent with boys might recognize this experience:

A mother and grandmother enter the cafe with five children for a snack—two girls and three boys, all between the ages of five and eight. "Now sit down and wait and I'll get you your treats," says the mother. The girls sit down at one small table with the grandmother and the boys go to another nearby. The girls gaze intently as their grandmother shows them one of her rings and describes how it was given to her by their grandpa, who is "in heaven" now. The girls ask questions and listen as the older woman answers. She doesn't finish, however, as she is distracted by the boys, who are jostling each other at the other table. "Now you boys sit back down!"

They become so loud that the grandmother says again, "You boys don't be rude or you won't get a treat!"

This appears to have little effect on the trio. The mother returns with a bag and says to the boys, "Here are your cookies, but you can't have them unless you sit down." They quickly sit down.

The mother turns to the girls, who wait while she doles out the goodies. As she's handing the cookie to the last girl, the mother is surprised, as one of the boys has come over and reached into the bag from behind. Trying to take his cookie, he cries, "Want mine!"

She pulls the bag away. "What did I say? Sit down!" He sullenly sits and the boys are given their cookies. They sit quietly for a moment and chow down, while the mother joins the grandmother and girls at their table. They chat about what they are going to do afterward and the girls listen, asking questions.

The boys are no longer quiet; they are not even at the table anymore. They are wandering around the café, cookies in hand, touching the various displays. They start to struggle over a package of coffee, cookies in one hand and package in the other, until one wins the battle and the other one cries, "TOBY! You said mine!"

Both the mother and grandmother look over.

"Boys, I told you to sit down—now do it! If you don't behave we aren't going to the park after!" says the mother, slightly exasperated.

The boys slouch toward their table.

"But Toby took mine!"

"Did not!"

The scene continues for a few minutes until the entire group leaves. My guess is that they headed for the park—because everyone needed a break!

If the differences between boys and girls are so profound during this simple outing, how much more evident will they be when you put large numbers of boys and girls together at school? If you visit the average kindergarten play area almost anywhere in North America, you will find children using their free time to do what they are attracted to and what gives them joy. By and large, you will see children self-segregated into gender groups, the boys playing with objects and using those objects as tools to mediate their relationships (e.g., in a soccer game), and the girls using their time to create imaginary social constructs. You will see girls talking much more than boys and moderating their behavior based on the feedback they receive verbally. Boys will also be communicating and moderating their behavior, but their interaction will would be based more on visual cues and physical experience. This generalized picture is the result of the differences between male and female brains. Educational practices that don't take into account these differences will not be effective for most boys; for some, they will even be tragic.

The 6 Secrets for Success

The six secrets in this book have the proven ability to foster a boy's motivated engagement and to leverage his discretionary effort. They are:

1. Movement
2. Game
3. Humor
4. Challenge
5. Mastery
6. Meaning

Illustrated, they can appear like this:

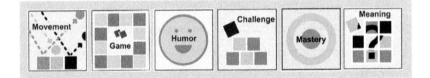

Each of these approaches can generate profound motivation in boys, as well as greater passion and attachment to their learning. But they are not all equal in importance. Their relation to each other is clearer in the following HBL (Helping Boys Learn) "secret target" image:

HBL Secret Target Tool™

They are arranged in concentric circles because, through wise guidance, parents and teachers can easily meet boys in the outer rings and lead them to the deeply satisfying and productive learning at the center. When that happens, motivation problems disappear, and boys are able to realize their potential for personal growth and contribution—at home, in class, and, ultimately, in society at large.

Not All Boys and Girls Are the Same: Important Considerations

While there are some generalizations such as the café story throughout *Helping Boys Learn*, they are generalizations borne of my research and experience. But it is also clear that all human behavior exists on continuum. Are all boys alike? Of course not. Are there girls who are more like boys than they are like other girls? In some cases, the answer is yes. As we shall see, the male and female brains do not universally exist solely in one gender. Brain researcher Michael Gurian describes his findings identifying the continuum within which all children's brains fall. Twenty percent of girls and 14% of boys have "bridge brains" that contain strong characteristics of the opposite gender's brain. Because of this, some of the ideas in this book may not work as well with boys you know—or they might work very well with some girls! Another factor to consider is that the differences between brains is most pronounced when children are younger. Through age and experience, male and female brains become increasingly similar, but that similarity is usually not present in school-aged children, who are fitted with what could be called the "factory model" brains. It is these brains that we must teach, and not only the "subjects" of school, but the lessons of passion of learning, understanding, commitment and resilience! Let's see how these secrets apply to the boys in your life...

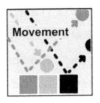

Boys Learn Where the Action Is

Why movement is so powerful for engagement and understanding in males

"Nothing happens until something moves."
—Albert Einstein

"I don't know what his problem is!" said the exasperated grade 3 teacher. "We just had recess and still he can't sit still. I don't think his rear end has touched the chair for more than a few minutes all year. He's constantly fidgeting and distracted and he distracts others as well! He's not a bad kid, really, but I have to admit that the days when he's absent are good days for me—days when the class seems more focused and on task. The only time he seems to slow down is when he's on the computer playing the video games. But even then he's still in motion, moving his hands, twitching his body and reacting to the game. Now I know the computer games I have in class are educational, but he can't do that all day!"

His teacher's cri de coeur is familiar to teachers everywhere. There are some kids who seem to be in constant motion, and the majority of them are boys (or girls who have the "male brains" described earlier). It is fairly easy to observe from our experience that boys love movement, whether it be the movement of their bodies in physical games or watching the movement of objects through space.

From the very beginning of their lives, boys pay more attention to movement than girls. One study of newborns gave babies the opportunity to look at a smiling live female face or a mobile (a small metal children's toy that rotates).. Boys almost always chose the mobile over the face, whereas girls did the opposite. This may be surprising, considering the female form provides the boy with food and loving attention, but it points out some important differences in male and female brain wiring. Movement strongly attracts boys. Their play almost always provides more dynamic movement than girl play. Boys are more easily distracted by movement, and they enjoy watching movement more than girls. Even as adults, physical and visual movement is more stimulating and pleasurable to men than it is to women.

In school, the male love of movement is a double-edged sword. Apart from the problems boys often have settling down and sitting still in class, the vast majority of discipline offenses committed by male students are movement-related: pushing, hitting, fighting, throwing objects, destroying school property, or running in the halls, to name a few. This is not so with female students, who are disciplined less often and for offenses that tend to be more verbal in nature. Yet the athletic triumphs that often make schools so proud and foster school spirit are full of action and movement—and boys are the ones who most often participate in them.

As a principal, I was often in negotiation with teachers, coaches, and parents to figure out a way to discipline a boy who committed a "movement offense" (e.g., throwing things in class) in such a way that he did not have to be suspended from the basketball team, which relied heavily on his movement-related skills to help them win games. One can debate whether it is appropriate to cater to boys' desires and talents for movement in such situations, but I point out the dilemma to demonstrate that movement is an important part of male existence that influences school behavior.

Typically, this love of movement in young males has been channeled into games and sports, whether in school or out. More males than females participate in sports and extracurricular activities involving movement, particularly dynamic movement with quick changes of pace and tempo. Indeed, this trend is apparent throughout life. Despite the clear male love of activities that allow physical movement, there is also a seeming paradox, which the teacher above alluded to: Many boys who can't sit still in class will remain motionless for hours when playing video games—except for finger twitching! The same holds true when they are engrossed in watching television or a movie. This inconsistency is explained by what they're watching: In almost all cases, it involves movement and action. Popular culture also reflects males' attraction to movement. Males gravitate toward movies containing more movement, whether they are action films or not, while those classified as "chick flicks"— because the predominant audience is female—have less movement. Video games and online activities that males enjoy also reflect a high degree of movement. The most popular sporting events marketed to males in the media are saturated with it.

It may be helpful to look at some of the characteristics of male movement before investigating why they are attracted to it. Everyone moves and enjoys movement, but particular types of movement appear to appeal more to boys than girls. Male-oriented movement is usually:

- *Dynamic* – Starting and stopping quickly, sometimes containing a great deal of power
- *Directed* – It has a purpose, and generally stops once it has achieved that purpose

- *Distanced* – It may take place over larger areas of space
- *Dependent* – It relies on male interaction with objects or others moving through space and involving contact and impact—sometimes violent

These qualities of movement are hard-wired in the male brain, and understanding them can provide a great pathway to meet boys in a place where they are ready to learn.

Why movement helps boys to learn

Research reveals that young boys' brains develop a tremendous amount of neural wiring to facilitate movement, the perception of movement, and a sensitivity for how things "fit" together. This wiring is situated on the right side of the brain and can become the determining factor in what the male brain easily pays attention to in any given situation. This neural wiring explains why newborn male babies will pay more attention to a mobile above the crib than to a live face looking at them—there's more movement on the mobile. However, if the head with the face starts making more exaggerated expressions and nodding up and down—particularly dynamically—the boy will automatically redirect his attention.

If you are the parent of a boy, particularly one younger than seven, it is often easy to see the effects of this wiring. Observe how easily he is distracted by movement, how much he enjoys looking around and watching what happens when he moves, when he makes objects move, and what type of movement occurs when he throws or pushes one thing into another. We might prefer that he does this with a ball or truck, and not his little brother—but what happens in his brain is the same! After working with young boys for many years, it's my impression that much of what is labeled as a tendency toward violence is actually the result of trying to discover and enjoy the kind of movement that happens when objects collide. It lights up the neural wiring of boys to see things roll, zoom, fly, crash, fall, tumble, explode, and, in general, "get blowed up real good!" More important, this desire to make use of their neural wiring for movement forms the basis for many boys' relationships to other people and to learning. In practice, understanding how movement affects the male brain can be a tremendous asset to parents who want to help boys learn effectively and enthusiastically.

All of this extensive wiring comes at a price for young boys. We know that language in both sexes is primarily rooted in the left side of the brain, and male brains do not develop this side as quickly as girls'. But on the right side of the female brain, where males have their "movement" wiring, the females do not; instead, they have enhanced wiring for language—both in speaking and listening. This explains why females typically develop language skills earlier than boys, have a wider vocabulary, and tend to speak, listen, and read more than boys throughout their lives. It is easy to see how these differences in wiring can have profound effects on learning in school for both genders.

The difference in brain wiring also affects how the brain is activated and maintains focus. When at rest, brain scans have shown much more activity in girls' brains than boys. A young girl , without even realizing it, uses more of her frontal lobes to perceive her environment, thinks in a detailed vocabulary, and express her thoughts with great complexity On the other hand, a young boy's brain at rest has activity primarily in the brain stem area, the most primitive part of the brain devoted to keeping the body breathing, digesting, etc. There is much less activity in the frontal lobes. When he perceives or takes part in movement, his brain becomes more active. Notice how males of all ages often pace more while talking on the phone, or move about when thinking, planning, or even preparing to write. My own surveys of both young and old learners have revealed that males often lose attention and focus earlier than females, that movement helps in boys' ability to focus.

In addition to that, boys—particularly younger boys—use dependent-contact movement with other boys to communicate. Pushing, shoving, wrestling, and grabbing are often the ways to wordlessly, but effectively, communicate their friendship. I have watched boys who are deeply engaged in planning a school assignment grabbing each other as if they were locked in combat, but neither of them minded. It was as if their bodily positions were essential to their understanding and communication while completing the task. Conversely, as a principal I disciplined many boys who made the mistake of showing a girl they "liked" her by punching her. The types of movement that would interrupt a girl's relationship with other girls—contact movement that is sharp, harsh, aggressive, and sometimes painful—can actually strengthen boys' relationships.

Why should this difference in neural wiring and behavior exist? It is most likely that they reflect the gender roles our ancestors played for millennia. Males were hunter-gatherers, and life and death depended on being able to read the environment for the movement of animals. Being able to move quickly to either attack (fight) and claim a food source or escape (flight) from danger was an evolutionary imperative. So was spatial-geographic sensitivity (it was important to know how far an animal was from you before you threw that spear). The neural wiring to support these tasks was refined over thousands of years, as was the development of stronger male musculature and the endurance required for intense bouts of physical activity and effort. The stress of hunting was followed by long periods of little activity for males—except for games of physical contact that improved hunting skills. Words were used infrequently, except to regale others with one's physical prowess.

Females, on the other hand, were in charge of keeping the home and children. They had slighter physical builds, and they needed to pay attention to their environment for more subtle changes, not least of which were the telltale signs that the males with whom a female interacted might turn violent and endanger her or her offspring. These needs developed the female ability to pay attention to small details and cues in the social environment, to negotiate with words to defuse conflict, and the skills needed to build social alliances with other women.

At first glance, these differences appear to have little relevance to our modern situation. After all, we don't live in primitive societies with the division of labor described. Our culture is much less violent and misogynistic. Women and men do most of the same jobs today, and we raise our children differently than in days gone by. Indeed, research shows that as we age, the differences in male/female brain wiring are greatly reduced, so that all 40-year-old brains are much the same. But much of the important brainwork for humans in regard to how we learn (and how we see learning) occurs when we're young, and our brains more readily reflect the primitive evolutionary experiences of our ancestors. It does not mean that biology is destiny, but it does help us explain why young boys have a need for movement and why it can serve as a useful tool to help boys learn the things we need them to learn for success in the 21st century.

Movement and school

When a boy is a toddler, we would never think of making him sit still for extended periods of time except in rare instances when it was necessary for his safety. But when he starts school, this is often the rule. There may be a great deal of movement allowed in kindergarten, depending on the setting, but in grade school this quickly changes; sitting still is required for the majority of the time he's there so he can "learn." Movement is restricted to recess and physical education, with some class movement allowed when absolutely necessary—suggesting that the learning required by school can only be effectively taught in a static environment. If a boy does not learn to sit down, listen, read and write at a desk, he will not be successful. But, as we have seen, this is counterintuitive to how his brain is wired. It results in a less effective learning environment for the male brain, particularly in those boys whose learning style is heavily kinesthetic (movement-based).

In an environment where movement is forbidden, boys' natural tendencies become behavior offenses. This situation can cause many problems at school and home. As we shall see, boys like challenges and games, and if movement is turned into a "rebel" activity, it will often surface in extreme forms, such as throwing, rolling, pushing, punching, etc. In essence, the evolutionary fight-or-flight response is triggered. If a boy does not consciously push back against the restriction on movement, he can be seen unconsciously fidgeting, twitching, pencil-tapping, bouncing, and swaying in class. Because their neural wiring makes them so aware of movement, many other boys can also be distracted by a single boy's fidgeting.

This is not the worst effect. For many boys, the "flight" response kicks in. Their brains go to the resting state that we saw in Figure 2. We know that school learning must involve the frontal lobes of the brain, the ones that evolved specifically to support higher-level thinking. Yet these are not in use when the brain, in effect, "goes to sleep." Sleeping brains may not appear obvious when you look in a classroom and see children sitting quietly in their desks, looking at the teacher, appearing to be engaged in the lesson. However, this is where the difference in male and female brain wiring can be most profound. Dr. Leonard Sax has compiled research asserting that because of these gender differences, boys enter school on average 18 months behind girls in their development of "oral language" skills—those responsible for the ability to speak and understand effectively. That's a tremendous difference for children who are only 4 to 5 years old. Oral language is the foundation for the vital skills of reading and writing. If this initial deficit is not corrected, a boy can fall behind his peers for the rest of his school life. When a boy's brain goes to sleep due to lack of engagement, his fidgeting and distracting are often efforts to re-engage his brain, but these actions can make people think that he is trying to not to pay attention! The classroom norm of sitting, talking, and listening is hard for many boys, but it is much easier for girl because they are processing language with greater neural wiring. The result is that girls often carry the in-class conversation with ease and skill and those boys who need to speak more to improve their oral language skills don't get the chance.

This difference in oral language abilities is very important for a parent to understand—especially when your son is young and in his first five years of school. Many parents of boys this age are told their child is "falling behind," or cannot focus, or cannot sit still and "respect" the rest of the children. However, a parent or teacher may not see that these things are all related to how movement helps him learn. So what is a physical need becomes a learning disability—or worse: a character flaw! Statistically, the teacher is most likely a female and therefore has never had any problem with oral language; indeed, her position in education is strong evidence that her oral language skills were not only just good, they were exceptional. This resulted in superior performance in reading, writing, and other educational tasks to such an extent that she decided to make her success in education the basis for a career. Unless she understands the brain science that explains why the boys in her class speak less and move more, she may believe their lack of language skills, distractibility, and tendency to fidget are evidence of things like poor socialization, poor parenting, laziness, an attention deficit disorder, immaturity, or a learning disability. This will prevent her from being able to leverage the power of movement to help the boys in her class learn better and improve their oral language.

Most important, the teacher or parent's attitude toward movement will have a profound impact on the attitude that many boys take toward classroom learning. Because movement has been a valuable tool in their learning prior to school, little boys innately trust its value. That trust supports their willingness to take risks and develop mastery in movement. As we shall see in later chapters, risk-taking and mastery are vital to boys' learning and their willingness to persevere in challenging situations and to build on strengths and previous successes. But success may be elusive for a little boy in a classroom where movement is not valued.

Even consistently gentle reminders from the teacher, telling a boy to sit still or praising those students (usually girls) who are able to do so, quickly sends the message to a boy that his strengths are not valued in this context. Dr. Sax has described how approaches like allowing the boys to "play" on their own in the classroom, while the teacher spends time with the girls who can sit still on the carpet, sends a clear message both about what the teacher values and about boys' inability to "make the grade." It is not surprising, then, that this inability is reflected in boys' actual grades as they progress through school.

All of this could be easily remedied if we used boys' movement strengths to help them practice and improve their oral language skills. This missed opportunity in the earliest years of schooling has unfortunate consequences. The use of either movement or oral language in the classroom tends to decrease progressively throughout grades 1 through 8 and even more in high school. Curriculum tasks grow more complicated, involving more individual reading and writing. Boys who have not yet mastered reading and writing because of their poor oral language skills are left behind. If a boy has not developed a solid base in oral language by around grade 3, the likelihood of his being able to catch up is reduced simply because of the reduced rate of "practice time" for him in the later grades.

Another physiological factor also comes into play around ages 6 and 7. Boys begin to have a greater release of testosterone, which has been largely dormant since it was released in great amounts in utero. They have even more desire to move aggressively, precisely when the classroom is reducing the amount of movement and requiring more challenging tasks like reading and writing. Those of us who have worked with children from ages 7 to 12 have observed how agitated boys can become when they are deprived of the opportunity to move and how important recess is to them. They spend much of the time leading up to recess anticipating it. Afterwards, they lament its end and relive the grand adventures (most of which involve a lot of movement) that filled their 15 minutes of freedom. Studies have shown that movement provides a tremendous stress relief for boys and can do so whether it's physical or video game-based. Many schools have recognized the value of movement in this way by encouraging daily physical activity in the form of 15-minute "body breaks."

Using movement to help boys learn

We have discovered through our work with thousands of boys that when movement is integrated into learning, the results are impressive: Boys learn with more motivation and joy, understand the material better, and achieve higher with greater success. Below are a few simple ways accomplish this:

MOVEMENT FOR LEARNING AT HOME

1. Walk and talk – One of the simplest ways for a parent to use movement to help a boy learn is to use it with speaking and learning. Taking a walk and discussing what your son learned at school can be an amazingly easy way to get him to talk about his learning and how he understands it. It can be done with homework as well, where you walk with him and review spelling words or the multiplication table. If a child is not in school yet, take "discover" walks into the woods or around the neighborhood and then talk about what he finds interesting. Ask him not just to identify something he finds interesting, but to explain it with questions like:

To see a video of a mom and her son doing "walk and talk," go to helpingboyslearn.com and enter M1 in the HBL TIP BOX.

- Why do you think it's like that?
- How do you think it got that way?
- What do you think will happen to it?
- Would you like to be a _____? Why?

2. "Show, tell, record" – This is a sequence that can be used anytime you want to engage a boy with joy and understanding. It can be done alone with your son, with his siblings, or with a group of his friends. Before talking about a topic, ask him to show you by freezing in a physical position. Once he's in that position, ask him to explain what he's doing and why. Finally, have him write it down. You can even use this to complete a homework assignment.

Let's say there are vocabulary words and concepts your son has to review for a test on the water cycle. You say, "Show me a frozen picture of evaporation with your body!" He may sprawl out on the floor with his fingers and toes reaching skyward. Once he is there, ask him to explain what he is illustrating. Help him reduce it to one sentence. Then challenge him to write that sentence quickly. As you do this for each part of the water cycle, you are building a study sheet that he not only can speak about but has embodied as well. This invariably makes him more engaged with the subject matter and facilitates his success on the upcoming test. You can use this to develop literacy skills in younger children as well. Just take any topic and use the sequence. This can be done anywhere, such as in the kitchen while dinner is being prepared. If your son is not quite up to writing yet, he can draw a picture and you can write words for him to see afterward. This type of activity makes great entertainment for grandparents and relatives, while increasing your son's love of learning.

To see a video, go to helpingboyslearn.com and enter M2 in the HBL TIP BOX.

3. **Phone photo writing** – An extension of the learning game above is to have your son freeze in a position and then take a picture with a phone or tablet device. Send that to your son and ask him to write a description. This can then be shared with friends, relatives, or even teachers.

To see samples, go to helpingboyslearn.com and enter M3 in the HBL TIP BOX.

4. Use of movement supports – Providing boys with bouncy balls to sit on or stress balls to squeeze, or even simply allowing boys to stand at the table while working have also proven effective with many active boys at home. Supports like these can help boys stay on task while doing homework or studying for a test.

For examples, go to helpingboyslearn.com and enter M4 in the HBL TIP BOX.

5. Handy Memory – This technique uses movement but can be done while sitting. Simply ask your son to create a hand movement that illustrates what he is learning. At the same time, he needs to speak while completing the movement. This will allow him to leverage the neural wiring he has for *both* language and movement. For example, if he is learning about the characteristics of a triangle, it could be done as is illustrated below.

"A Triangle has..........three..........sides..........and three....... Vertices!"

For a detailed description, go to helpingboyslearn.com and enter M5 in the HBL TIP BOX.

MOVEMENT IN THE CLASSROOM

Movement is already used as a tool to support boys in school, but not often for learning. It is seen as a break (recess), physical fitness (physical education, activity breaks), or a reward (going to the gym or outside when classwork is done). It is also a community/character builder (house leagues, sport teams, drama, and dance). These activities are all valuable and make a school environment a better place for boys. However, few of the present approaches leverage the tremendous potential that movement can provide for engagement and understanding when used with the daily work in the classroom. Here are some of the most effective strategies:

1. **Don't spend more than 30 minutes on static learning** – We know that there are diminishing returns even for adults at this point, so it's important to be aware of how much time has passed.

2. **Focus on the work—not the wiggling!** – We have seen that boys use movement to reengage their brains. Allowing a place in class (preferably at the back) where they can stand, move, crouch, or practice other movements while they do their work is acceptable as long as they do not abuse the allowance and distract those who find sitting still the better way to learn. The important thing to pay attention to is not how they are moving, but their productivity.

3. **Use movement supports as necessary** – Allowing bouncy balls to sit on and providing squeeze (or stress) balls is helpful; even simply allowing boys to stand at their desks while working has proven effective with many active boys.

4. **Link speaking and listening to movement** – As described in the previous section, having boys move at the same time they

are discussing a topic is very powerful. If they use their bodies to illustrate a concept and then describe why they chose those movements, they experience greater engagement and deeper understanding of the material being discussed. Using "frozen picture" or "slow-motion" movement are easy ways to accomplish this.

5. **Progress from movement to writing** – Having boys use their bodies to illustrate their speech before writing has proven to be one of the most effective ways to help boys write well because they are much better able to visualize what they will be writing about.

If you would like to share an expanded list of movement strategies for the classroom with your son's teacher, you can download the teacher tip sheet at helpingboyslearn.com and enter MT in the HBL TIP BOX.

Boys Learn in the Game

The power of playing with knowledge…

"Even when I'm old and grey, I won't be able to play it, but I'll still love the game."
—Michael Jordan

The middle school classroom was quiet as students worked on their assignment. The dismissal bell was five minutes away. Jamal looked down at his book and was writing furiously, but his scribbling of x's and o's would have seemed like an odd way to answer the literature questions he was assigned. That's because he was diagramming soccer plays he was planning to suggest to the coach at tonight's practice. He had just come up with a perfect play, one that he knew no one in the school's league could defend against, when he sensed someone watching him. He looked up and noticed Mr. Fonseca, his teacher, standing next to him.

"Jamal, have you finished the questions yet?" he asked.

Sliding his diagram under his book, Jamal replied, "No sir, but I'm working on them—I'm going to finish them tonight."

"It doesn't look like it…" said the teacher, picking up the assignment sheet that had only one of the 10 questions answered. He knew Jamal was thinking about soccer again, and he knew that his likelihood of doing any more after school was nil. "I think we'd better chat after class."

"But sir, I've got practice!" Jamal stammered.

"We'll see about that. Your schoolwork comes first."

As he moved away from a now-angry Jamal, the bell rang. Mr. Fonseca braced himself for another uninspiring talk with the boy, trying to get him to see the importance of working hard and achieving in school for his future. The teacher knew that throughout it all, Jamal would nod and promise to do anything, as long as he could escape to soccer practice as soon as possible. Mr. Fonseca was doing his job, but he sensed that no matter how convincing he was, or even how interesting his lectures or class material were, he would never be able to compete with *the game*.

Games have been loved by males since the beginning of time. Today, professional sports alone comprise a more than $600 billion industry. Males participate in and love the majority of these games. It is undoubtedly true that females love games as well, but boys play them with an intensity and investment of self that can border on the ridiculous to most girls. It is not often you see two 8-year-old girls rolling on the floor, physically fighting because one of them beat the other in a video game, but parents of male siblings close in age can easily remember such an instance. A frustrated mother, separating the combatants, might shake her head and chide, "What's wrong with you?! It's just a game!" But somehow it seems more than that to the boys.

We saw in the previous chapter how important movement is for boys. The vast majority of organized movement activities that boys participate in are built around games. While many girls might be quite happy to participate in a group or a dance class where there is movement but no game or competition, most boys would not. They want more than being *with* each other: they want to play *against* each other.

The game becomes the organizing principle for much of boys' social lives.

Boys will play games even when no one else is around. Leonard Sax describes an experiment where they placed individuals in a room and gave them plastic rings. They also gave them a small plastic post and asked the subjects to place the rings on the post. This puzzled many of the participants who asked if they were supposed to do anything else. But there were no other requirements; they were simply to toss the rings on the post. Researchers then observed what happened when they left the subjects alone with the rings. Almost all of the females looked at the rings, tossed them on the post from a short distance away, and then sat down and waited for the researcher to return. Not one male did this! All of them started to toss the rings on the post, moving farther away each time in an effort to see how far away they could stand and still hit the post. The activity was not complete for these males without it becoming a game.

Many times a single game is not enough for boys—they prefer to have games with multiple levels of complexity. A great example of this is the popular television show *Pardon the Interruption*, or "PTI" to its legions of male viewers. In this program, two sports columnists discuss the major sports issues of the day, often arguing about them. Their disagreements are best described as a game, where one tries to show how wrong the other is. But the game is elevated even further by the timer that appears in corner of the screen as they talk. There are only 30-60 seconds allocated to each subject and they must get all of their arguments in before the timer counts down to zero. Once the bell rings and time is up, they immediately switch to another subject. There is even a referee who appears near the end of the show and tells them how many factual mistakes were in their session, awarding extra points to the winner. This style of social discourse is not replicated in any program designed to appeal to females. It would seem stupid to most women to have to jam everything they want to say about something into 30-second blocks, and then keep score of the mistakes they made. Can you imagine, say, an episode of Oprah that did that? It would be insulting to the guests and cheapen the conversation. Yet, for boys and many men, the experience of the conversation is heightened and rendered more enjoyable in the context of a "boys' game."

The games boys like contain important characteristics that help us understand why they help boys learn. Male-oriented games are usually:

1. **Competitive challenges** – They test the boys' efforts against something or someone in an effort to achieve a goal. In doing so, games can provide effective ways for boys to experience *challenge, mastery,* and *meaning,* which, as we shall see later in the book, are vital for their learning.

2. **Counted and counting** – They involve keeping score or track of how successful the efforts expended in the game have been. Counting the results proves to males that the task is important and worthy of being taken seriously.

3. **Clearly defined (rule-based)** – They have a beginning and an end. The rules help the participant play the game correctly. Often an authority figure or referee helps resolve disputes over the rules. In male games, clearly defined and predetermined rules are important because they show boys the parameter of acceptable ways to compete. They outline when the game starts and finishes and how success is determined. Even when a boy is penalized for breaking the rules, he is comforted by those rules because they help him see the way to success and, indeed, mastery. Later we will see how important a pathway to mastery is for boys, and game rules subtly provide that.

4. **Connecting him to others** – Games mediate social relationships for boys. They provide spaces for males to use their
   competitive instincts to build bonds, friendship and selfless
   behavior, by allowing for indirect communication between the
   participants and the sublimation of the ego for a larger goal.

When boys "play," they most often choose male games that have
one or more of these characteristics. These games can be irresistible to
most boys because they open pathways to knowing their environments,
knowing others, and, most important, knowing themselves. Let's look
a little deeper at what makes games so appealing to male brains.

Why games help boys to learn

We have seen how boys' brains are wired differently to cause
them to move and perceive movement so that they could survive and
thrive in primitive times. Games evolved in the same way, providing
a safe place to hone their survival skills in demonstrations of physical and mental prowess. These competitions leveraged effective use of
the amygdala, a small part of the brain at the base of the skull that
releases neurotransmitters, alerting humans to danger. It is a very powerful contributor to emotional learning, triggering the fight-or-flight
impulse. Since the games were designed to help hunters in the "fight,"
as males evolved, the amygdala became extremely sensitive to the
challenges of competitive games, simulating in males the stresses that
could be associated with the actual dangers of the hunt. This could be
one reason that the amygdala is larger in males and is used to process
emotions more quickly than the core complex parts of the brain that
females often use to process emotions.

Because of this, males tend to have intense emotional attach-
ments to games that are very stressful to the male body and psyche.
Games were often structured to foster intense focus and drive par-

ticipants toward the goal within short periods of time. Research has demonstrated that when faced with the moderate stress caused by a timed task, most boys are able to focus and perform better, whereas most girls do not. It again harkens back to our past; successful hunting required intense action at the right time for ancient males, while sustained action with moderate intensity over longer periods of time was essential for the life skills of females. Each gender evolved wiring a brain function to help perform their roles with the most effectiveness, and it means that even today, most boys react well to the stress induced by time-restricted tasks.

We have long known that male sexuality is driven by testosterone, but modern brain research has revealed just how powerful testosterone can be elsewhere, particularly when connected with competition and games. Studies have demonstrated that when males are successful (i.e., they win the game), there is a spike in testosterone released. They feel it immediately and receive a tremendous sense of well-being. Conversely, when males are not successful (or they lose), they suffer a reduction in testosterone. They feel lousy and often try to get a win quickly to feel better. This understanding helps us appreciate a lot of the phenomena associated with males and competitive games, and supports understanding of the extreme reaction some boys have to winning and losing. While it can be made more acute by societal factors, it has a physiological basis that precedes any socialization. This would explain the generally observed male tendency to quit early or avoid games where they are not successful, and it makes sense when we understand how body chemistry changes when one "loses."

Watching a favorite sports team win can provide enough vicarious attachment to winning to trigger the release of testosterone. This is why many males are so passionately attached to "their" teams. Video games, where the game usually contains a lot of movement and allows winning in structured and adjustable steps, provide boys with easy access to testosterone-induced "highs" within a protective framework. Indeed, video game creators are increasingly aware of this and take it into account as they design their games.

The arguments presented here are not an excuse for bad male behavior or perpetual immaturity in boys. However, male attachment to games is hard-wired and needs to be considered if we want to help them learn more effectively. School is about mastering the information and skills needed to learn, and games provide a natural way to achieve mastery while motivating boys to undertake the tasks necessary for achievement. By tapping into their love of play, games naturally engage boys.

It is interesting to note that the love of play is also observed in other species. In my previous book, I described a true story from Play by Dr. Stuart Brown. He related how a team of sled dogs in the far north encountered a gaunt and hungry bear one afternoon. The bear moved toward the dogs, appearing ready to attack. One of the dogs, upon seeing the bear approach, adopted a playful stance with his back arched, paws out in front and ears back. The bear stopped and then proceeded to play with the dog for the next half hour, rolling around in the snow with wild abandon. The bear returned every evening for the next week to do the same, before finally disappearing—presumably to continue his search for food. This power of play is used to spur learning in a variety of ways. The wrestling of lion cubs may appear "cute," but it is vital for developing their hunting skills. Dr. Brown has described how it provides improvisational skills in an ever-changing environment for bears and the ability to socialize for cats. He writes, "Play is nature's greatest tool for creating new neural networks and for reconciling cognitive difficulties."

Games and school

Boys' love of games can significantly disrupt classroom learning for themselves and others. As illustrated in Jamal's example, the most basic of these disruptions is the thoughts and daydreams associated with pleasurable game experiences that take a boy's mind away from the classroom. On the day of a big game or competition in particular, he may have considerable trouble focusing on the teacher and his coursework. Beyond extracurricular games, however, boys often want to turn everything into a game. I have seen this form the basis of any number of classroom "discipline" problems. Here's a typical example:

Mrs. Casion has just asked the class to move into their work groups for science, and Chan and Morris both race for the same chair, trying to shove each other off and then fighting about it. "He's taking my chair, Mrs. C!" calls out Morris.

"Did not, I was here first! Tell him to get another one."

Trying to minimize the distraction because they only have 20 minutes for the experiment, Mrs. Casion says, "Morris, just take another seat."

"Oh, man, teacher's pet!" Morris sneers to a triumphantly smiling Chan, but not before he punches him while walking to another chair.

"Oww!" whines Chan in an exaggerated manner. "Ma'am, did you see what he did!?"

"*Enough!*" barks Mrs. Casion, irritated. "You're going to the principal's office if this doesn't stop right now." The boys settle down and the teacher begins to direct the class in the experiment, not noticing the sly smile exchanged between the boys. They have just briefly satisfied their "male game" need.

Two boys flicking small objects at one another or a third student, asking to go to the washroom at the same time, making faces and bodily noises, stacking items on the desk, or seeing how long it takes to get another student to yell "Cut it out!"—these are all examples of game playing that can go on in class. If you examined them, you would find that even though they only last a moment or two, they would have the male game characteristics of competition, counting, and connection, with the rules being implied and tacitly understood. It is interesting to note that a classroom disruption is sometimes an appeal to the unwitting teacher to become the referee in a game and clarify the rules or the winner, and that is exactly what happened to Mrs. Casion in the chair game played by Chan and Morris.

A darker side of game playing can be the escalation of a game into hyper-competitiveness in boys who already have low self-esteem. This is often connected to an inappropriate attempt to satisfy a male's need for mastery. I'll describe why this occurs later, but it is seen when a simple game or competition becomes a seeming life-or-death matter, and a boy doesn't just want to win the game, but wants to crush and humiliate other players. The disruption and emotional toll this can have on children can cause teachers to avoid using games in their classes. This negative effect of games can be felt, however, even when the game does not take place in the classroom. A hyper-competitive boy who has lost a game at recess will often sulk for the next class period, getting little work done and fighting with his classmates and the teacher.

Because boys' love of games is so powerful, it has often been held over their heads by parents and teachers to leverage school achievement. Boys are not allowed to play on teams, go to recess, or participate in gym if their behavior and schoolwork are not satisfactory. As a teacher, principal, and parent of two boys, I did this myself, but am less confident of its benefits now. It did seem to leverage more accomplishment in school, but it was compliance accomplishment and not the engaged accomplishment that research has shown creates the most effective learning. In fact, such consequences probably created more neural pathways with negative association to school and classroom learning, because schoolwork was always perceived as something standing in the way of the joy and learning that was natural to the game experience.

When school learning and games are set up as opposites in this fashion, it is ultimately not helpful. If school learning becomes something that not only makes a boy's life miserable in class but after school as well, it does not create a good foundation for the type of passionate engagement in classroom learning that has been demonstrated to bring lifelong benefits. It makes much more sense to help satisfy the desire for games both in and outside of class, with the goal of using the profound learning that can be found through games to bring joy and passion to a boy's approach to school, learning, and achievement.

Using games to help boys learn

When considering educational games, the first thing we may think of is video and online games for boys' learning or "learning games" that you can buy at the store. These resources exist, but their usefulness for boys' learning varies depending on the content and approach. They have a place for learning both at home and school, but should be evaluated by how they contribute to growth in light of the six secrets of boys' learning in this book. However, parents can use the knowledge in this book to create their own games that help boys become engaged, passionate, and successful in learning—whether at home or school. All that is needed is the application of the Helping Boys Learn framework. Let's examine some ways to apply that framework

GAMES FOR LEARNING AT HOME

Toss and Talk – This is a great game for boys because it also uses their attraction to movement. It can be done at any time and with anything they need to learn. All you need is a ball, pillow, bean bag, or other small toy—something softer than a baseball is best! You and your son toss the object back and forth, throwing it only when one of you can say a newly learned fact. For example, if you are learning colors with a boy between the ages of three and six, you only toss the ball each time one of you can name a color. If it's a boy in kindergarten through third grade and you are reviewing math definitions for homework, the sequence could go as follows:

BOY (Holding ball): "A triangle has 3 sides and three vertices!" (Tosses ball to PARENT)

PARENT: (Catches ball): "What is the distance around the triangle called?"

BOY: "Perimeter!" (PARENT tosses ball back)

To see a video, go to helpingboyslearn.com and enter G1 in the HBL TIP BOX.

This could go on for two or 20 minutes. It could be used as an oral review or in preparation for doing a homework assignment. The value lies in the fact that it triggers the boy's engaged motivation in math and improves his brain's neural connections, as well as his understanding around triangles!

To vary this activity so that it can be used frequently, focus on the four aspects of the game that make it so powerful for boys:

1. Competitive challenge – Once you have played toss and talk, you can make it more competitive in the following ways:

- See how many correct tosses can be done before a wrong answer stops the circuit.

- When you have the ball, have the boy ask you a question about the subject matter that you have to answer and he has to confirm as correct (or give the right answer himself) before the ball is tossed.
- Have the boy toss the ball up to himself and answer the question correctly before he catches it.

2. Counted and counting – This is best done visually—using a chart on the fridge or writing in a special notebook, for example. Rewards could be set for achievement related to the number of tosses. Keep track of how many tosses can be done before a wrong answer, the number of days in a row the talk and toss is played, or the number of different topics talk and toss is done for. Goals and rewards can be set if desired.

3. Clearly defined rules – This is where you can influence the outcome. For example, to keep an excited boy from throwing the object too hard or quickly, the toss must be done in a way that it is easy to catch, or else it is a "do over" (with a new piece of information required, of course!). Another rule could allow the boy to look up a piece of information from a book or set of notes when he's stumped or run out of ideas.

4. Connecting him to others – This is where a boy's siblings and friends can get involved. One of them takes your place but the rules are the same. If different children have different topics for homework, it works fine as long as each one answers the questions on the correct homework topic. As a matter of fact, your son would probably love asking questions to his older sister about her homework. This could be very important in giving him the innate understanding that he is smart enough to be "teacher" as well as sparking his interest in future school subject matter. Another great technique is to have your son review his schoolwork with classmates at home. For example, if his friends come over to play videos, make talk and toss a game they need to play (achieving a certain number of correct toss responses) before the video game is turned on.

Beat the Clock – You can help focus a boy on the learning at hand by remembering how time limits serve to increase his focus and intensity. Simply set a time frame for a task to be done and check on it when the time is up. The trick to this is knowing the appropriate amount of time needed for the task at hand. For boys who have not been successful in learning, too large a task within too little time will have the same effect as it did for a caveman on the Savannah who saw a wildebeest a half mile away—there would be no way he would try and capture it because he would not have the time to get there. However, if it were a rabbit in the thicket just ahead, *that* would be a different story.

To determine where the "rabbit" is for the boy in question, ask him how much time he thinks he will need to get a defined portion of a learning task done. For school-aged children, it's best to use a time frame of 15-30 minutes, but it can start for as little as 5 minutes, say, to answer one question from a textbook. Once he has agreed to a time, set the criteria for success (e.g., a complete sentence answer) and set a timer. If the task is completed within the criteria—even if it was done within a fraction of the time allotted—the boy should be given the full amount of time agreed upon, even if he uses it for other purposes, (e.g., drawing a picture or playing a short video game). Once he has finished the first part, ask him to estimate a total time for the rest of the tasks at hand and let him know that as long as he meets the criteria, he can do more to get it done sooner. Now we can use each of the characteristics of game to improve these timed efforts.

1. Competitive challenge – Some boys will enjoy the short effort followed by a relaxation sequence, but many will be happy they are "beating the clock" and will try to do it better. Remember, the blast of testosterone they get for winning can be very powerful for them. So once they have started beating the clock successfully, challenge them to improve either the time they take to complete similar tasks in the future or to improve the quality of what they complete, but within the same time frame. You could also ask them to identify other tasks they could do within the same amount of time and then try to complete them.

2. Counting and counted – Here you can focus on a number of things, as long as they are recorded visually. This will constantly remind him that he has succeeded in learning activities before, that he has been able to improve his performance over time—and that he can do it again! Things you can help him keep track of:

- How many tasks are performed in a time frame
- Number of successful timed sessions held in a week, month, etc.
- How many breaks were needed within the time frame
- Number of sessions started and stopped by the boy on his own—without parent nagging, etc.
- How his performance compares against siblings, friends, or classmates

To download a chart to graph progress or access a cool online charting tool, go to helpingboyslearn.com and enter G2 in the HBL TIP BOX.

3. Clearly defined rules – This is where you can set the criteria for completing a task so that a boy doesn't just rush through something to beat the clock while producing a poor result. As mentioned earlier, the secret here is starting with something that can be done well and relatively easily within the time frame and then carefully increasing the requirements or reducing the time needed, observing where the happy medium is between timed focus and good quality work. It will be different for each boy.

4. Connecting him to others – Inviting a boy's male classmates over to work on homework or learning tasks together within a Beat the Clock framework can be tremendously powerful for helping a boy develop collaborative skills and positive attitudes around school learning. As I will explain more fully in the mastery chapter, the use of a group to meet a common challenge is an integral part of team sports. For thousands of years, this activity has provided males with motivated engagement that triggers their discretionary effort. In a learning context, it reduces anxiety in struggling learners as they are not alone in facing problems. Tracking progress and providing simple rewards (like ice cream!) for successful group accomplishments, can be a small investment to gain a priceless return: your son's passionate engagement in learning.

Beat the Boss – Boys love winning against authority. So when challenged to win a game against an adult or supposed "expert," they find it hard to resist! They will focus and learn things they had no interest in previously if it allows them to triumph against a powerful and worthy opponent. As an adult or authority figure in your son's life, *you* can be that opponent.

1. *Competitive challenge* – One example of this is a game for learning spelling words with a parent. Once the boy has mastered one of the assigned spelling words, he can use a thesaurus to pick a word that means the same thing and ask the adult to spell it! Providing a small reward, like extra computer, TV, or video time each time the adult misspells a word, will get those spelling words learned in record time—along with a few synonyms to boot!

2. *Counted and counting* – Keep track of how often a boy wins. This can be recorded in ways listed previously, but also in the authority figure's public interaction with others. For example, a parent's Facebook page or Twitter feed could feature an update like: *"Today my son beat me in a contest about definitions related to growing plants! I better study up for the next game. ;)"* Getting friends and others to comment on your post reinforces the accomplishment the boy has made by learning and may provide some other authority figures to compete against!

3. *Clearly defined rules* – These may be simple, but should emphasize that to win the game the boy must demonstrate the knowledge that you are focused on having him learn.

4. *Connecting him to others* – This is a great opportunity for a boy to demonstrate his knowledge in a game against an outside authority. There are many online games and challenges that allow him to use what he is learning to win a game. Doing this together with a parent, grandparent, relative or friend increases his connectedness further.

To access an updated list of on-line games for different school subjects, go to helpingboyslearn.com and enter G3 in the HBL TIP BOX.

Beat the Best – Challenging themselves to achieve their personal best is the way that many people have accomplished amazing things throughout history. It is a game played against our inner sloth who would have us be less than we are capable.

Helping a boy find a way to challenge himself for school or homework tasks triggers his motivated engagement and discretionary effort because it meets the male need for mastery and meaning. It fosters self-discipline and accomplishment that can become a powerful tool for that boy for the rest of his life. More on this will be found in later chapters, but here are some simple ways to get started using it as a game .

1. *Competitive challenge* – Start with a learning task that he has already accomplished with ease. An example from the timed activity above would be to ask a boy who had accomplished his task well within the time, "So how quickly do you think you could do the next one, but still get it right and done neatly?" If he responds with a time, ask him why he doesn't see if he can do it, but add a bit of doubt into your voice. Even if he doesn't openly respond directly to your doubt, his ego will likely desire to set up competition to do just that!

2. *Counted and counting* – Once he has identified his goal, record it simply, along with the rules that define its accomplishment. Then display it in a place where the boy and others can see it, such as on the fridge.

3. *Clearly defined rules* – For Beat the Best to be successful, the boy must set the rules for the challenge himself. This is

one instance where the rules cannot be imposed from the outside. You can serve as a resource to help a boy define what needs to be done to meet the challenge of the game. In this role, it is important to help the boy choose a goal that is reasonable to accomplish within the time frame and criteria set out. Too easy is better than too hard. If

To access a simple online form that will allow you to record a challenge goal for a boy that can be printed and displayed, go to helpingboyslearn.com and enter G4 in the HBL TIP BOX.

he wants to choose something you think is too difficult or unreasonable, suggest that he break it down into levels, like those found in video games. As he progresses through each level, he will be better able to stay committed to meeting his challenge.

4. *Connecting him to others* – He should be encouraged to share his goal with others, such as his teacher, siblings, grandparents, or online friends and relatives. Their support validates his goal and reaffirms that others believe he can win the game he has constructed. However, it must be his choice to share. If he's hesitant to share before meeting his goal, respect his wishes. If he does meet his goal and win the game, ask him if it is OK to share his victory. He will most likely agree, and the feedback and recognition he gets will spur him on to create and meet other personal goals.

GAME IN THE CLASSROOM

Like movement, games are often a part of school life, but are not used to their full potential to support boys' learning. In the teachers' edition of Helping Boys Learn, I outline approaches and strategies similar to the ones you have seen above, but tweaked to make them directly applicable in a classroom setting.

If you would like to share with your son's teacher or principale some ways that game can help him learn, go to helpingboyslearn.com and enter GT in the HBL TIP BOX.

Boys Learn With Laughter

Taking humor seriously for male motivation

"One thing you have to remember, farts are always funny..."
—Anonymous male in Thomas
Newkirk's *Misreading Masculinity*

Mrs. Honderick looked around the circle and smiled warmly. On the carpet sat 14 kindergarten children, looking up at her expectantly. Everyone was ready to begin the morning routine. Well, not everyone... She furrowed her brow as she heard riotous giggling coming from the cloakroom. She did not have to guess who it was.

"Jason and Michael, the chime has been rung," she said in a voice loud enough for them to hear. The children in the circle looked at the small bell she used to call students to the carpet. The two boys did not appear, although the volume of their laughter rose.

"Boys, did you hear me?" she said with a bit of irritation in her voice. Still more guffawing, and now the other children on the carpet were looking at one other and starting to smile.

"All right, I'm counting down," the teacher said firmly. "3...2..."

Alerted to the fact that their recess time might be in jeopardy, the boys charged out of the coat area with broad smiles on their faces and ran toward the circle. They jumped into their spots in the circle, with Michael making the screeching sound of car wheels skidding as he landed in his place. This caused a number of the students in the circle—mostly boys—to giggle.

"Mrs. Honderick, the boys were running in class," a 5-year-old girl pointed out helpfully to the teacher.

"Yes, Hannah, I know." She thought about making them go back and walk, but that would just allow them more time to distract the class. She needed to get started and at least they were sitting now.

"Now boys, you know it's not polite to make the other children wait after I've rung the chime," she chided. "We have many exciting things to do today." As she turned to pick up the numbers for the daily calendar, she added almost as an afterthought, "I can't imagine what was so funny that you couldn't wait to share it with all of us."

Michael and Jason looked at each other as if they had won a jackpot and couldn't believe their luck. Mrs. Honderick realized her mistake the moment the words left her mouth, but before she could say anything else, Jason blurted out, "Michael said that my hand wasn't really my hand—it was my BUTT!" The class exploded in laughter, with many of the little bodies writhing on the floor at the hilarity of it.

"That's *enough!*" the teacher declared firmly. "You boys will behave yourselves and use appropriate language or you will be going to Mrs. Masterson's office!"

The class quieted quickly, sensing their teacher's anger and the threat of a visit to the school's principal. Jason and Michael did their best to appear chastened, putting their heads down, but their eyes still flashed mirthfully as they stole glances at each other.

Shaking her head gravely, Hannah declared, "Boys are sooo immature."

Many teachers and, indeed, many women throughout the centuries have wondered about the immaturity of males, particularly when it comes to humor. The word puerile, which means juvenile, silly, and childish, actually comes from the Latin word meaning "boy." Much of that juvenile silliness seems connected with a slapstick approach to bodily functions, gross images, painful mistakes, and even violence. It can appear to be insensitive, inappropriate, and even cruel—and it is not restricted to young males. We've seen the power that action movies with lots of movement have for male brains. Another genre of film and TV is devoted to what can be called "buddy comedy," which generates laughs through all of the puerile antics listed above, often with a crass approach to sexuality thrown in for good measure. To be sure, there are women who find this humor appealing, but its audience is primarily male.

On the other hand, males who have a "sense of humor" are seen by many females as more creative, intelligent, honest, and empathetic—not to mention more fun to be around. This is perhaps because male humor encompasses more than puerile aspects. Understanding this can help parents and teachers use the power and potential of humor to help boys learn and achieve at home and school. Let us examine the funny side of a boy's psyche more closely…

Why humor helps boys to learn

For all people, laughing has been shown to have important physiological benefits. It releases endorphins and dopamine, improves mood, moderates pain, improves social cohesion, increases creativity, and even improves memory. For males, however, like movement and games, humor can be an indirect communication tool as well. In the same way playing a game allows boys to express friendship, build camaraderie, and learn together while focusing on the activity, rendering something a joke or silly provides a "safe" place to explore male bonds and emotions.

Females more easily express their feelings in words because of their evolutionary drive to build relationships and the natural complexity of their neural wiring for speech. This allows their emotional processing to take place in the more advanced frontal lobes of the brain. Research has demonstrated that boys' emotions are processed initially in the more primitive parts of the brain and come more indirectly to the speech centers. That's why it's often so hard for many boys to orally express the complexity of their thoughts. But in the same way a "heart-to-heart" chat about feelings can bind women together, a crude joke that metaphorically captures the essence of something will achieve the same purpose for males. Essentially, it means *"We understand each other in this moment."*

Beyond providing a context for camaraderie, male humor helps engage and motivate boys. Slapstick and ridiculous physical comedy stimulate the right-brain neural wiring boys have for movement, and much of the cartoonish and violent humor in movies uses movement as the vehicle for laughs. But there is more to it, according to evolutionary theorist Alastair Clarke. He has written that the recognition of patterns was essential to the survival of primitive humans and that humor developed to help them deal with the surprise that occurs when a pattern is interrupted. In other words, we expect something to happen because we have seen it happen numerous times and, when it doesn't, it's funny. For males, whose neural wiring is designed to help them perceive changes in their environment, the surprise inherent in humor can re-engage them in a situation where their interest was flagging.

There is a deeper power for boys in humor, however: It is an effective tool for self-esteem when they feel challenged. Many of the things boys find funny are based on the reversal of power relationships. Boys have a need for mastery and control, and humor provides a refuge when they do not have either. It allows them to level the playing field and introduce equality. That's why someone slipping on the banana peel can be funny to a boy—the person who fell thought he was in control of himself and his world, but a simple piece of fruit brings him down. When the person brought down is in a position of arbitrary power over the boy, it is even more satisfying. It allows boys to say, *"You may have power, but you're not better than me."*

Thomas Newkirk writes that humor has always been used by those with less power to equalize the situation. It appears in schools because students are somewhere they don't necessarily want to be with little decision-making power over what happens. It allows for them to keep a distance from the institution while complying with its rules.

Humor also helps males when they are afraid. Remember how the amygdala can quickly trigger the fight-or-flight mechanism? Making a joke is a male technique for resisting or channeling that mechanism, turning perceived danger into a momentary unreality through laughter. Its extreme form is "gallows humor," where men make light of life-threatening situations, such as when former United States president Ronald Reagan remarked to surgeons trying to save his life after an assassination attempt, "I hope you're all Republicans." On Oscar Wilde's deathbed, he quipped, "Either that wallpaper goes—or I do." Less dramatically, it is an excellent way to relieve stress and can defuse potentially explosive situations between males.

When you take this attraction to humor and add the male love of competitive game, humor is then revealed as a sign of cleverness. Boys will vie to see who can be the best at using humor to relieve boredom, poke fun at the powerful, or display their fight-or-flight instinct in situations that they perceive as threatening.

Humor and school

Teachers often see male humor as a distraction or diversion from work in the classroom. It is something that might be fine in another place, but not in class. In the anecdote that opened this chapter, the two boys were being "silly," and their foolishness delayed the learning that was planned for that morning. Even worse, they infected others with their silliness. In his book Misreading Masculinity, Thomas Newkirk argues that this can be found in almost every classroom—it's like a "field of energy" that surrounds classrooms during self-determined and official breaks in sanctioned activity. Boys almost always instigate it, and teachers sometimes spend a great deal of time trying to keep a lid on the energy.

It becomes subversive when it introduces things that are forbidden in the classroom, like gross language or bathroom humor. The oral use of this kind of humor by boys is most frequent, but is also present in much of the creative writing they are asked to do in class. It may not seem very creative to most teachers or parents when it is a series of gags or crude events, strung together haphazardly without regard to storyline and included just because they seem funny to the boy who wrote it. But keep in mind, he's not writing for the adults. He knows that he has a ready-made audience for his literary efforts—his buddies!

Even more challenging for the teacher is when boys try to use humor to reverse the power relationship in class, where the teacher holds the authority and the students are subject to that authority. Implied or outright criticism of the teacher and learning can take different forms:

- Side jokes to friends that cause eruptions of laughter
- Saying something outrageous that a boy knows will force the teacher to discipline him or send him out of class

- Drawings, caricatures, or online pages that make fun of teachers

It is important to note that boys' use of humor to leverage power is not only directed upward toward the teacher. It can be used to establish the pecking order in a classroom and make sure those who are at the lower end of that order know it and stay put. A boy who wants to get attention can make a loud, cruel joke about another student and the laughter he receives enhances his social position. It is easy to see how this behavior can be considered bullying, since it diminishes the dignity of both students who are subjected to it as well as those who indulge in it.

Using humor to help boys learn

Male humor, contrary to first appearances, can have an extremely dark side in a school context. It is tempting to conclude that the best way to deal with it is to keep it to a minimum where learning is the priority. But like movement and game, humor can be extremely powerful in leveraging boys' motivated engagement and discretionary effort. Remember, the boy who writes the four-page comic story full of crude humor and puerile jokes has still written four pages! The trick is to leverage humor to help boys grow and become contributing members of the class as they mature. It is just as important to help boys see how humor can be an extremely powerful tool for success. Microsoft Corporation, perhaps not considered a company filled with hilarity, actually has outlined a humor competency for teachers on their education site:

Proficiency Level

Basic	Intermediate	Advanced	Expert
Generally uses humor in a positive way	Uses humor to bring people together	Knows exactly when and where a joke or story will be effective	Can see humor in almost everything
Is conscientious about timing and setting for humor	Uses humor to boost morale or decrease tension	Has a great sense of timing	Sought out by others for guidance in this area
Tries to defuse tense situations with appropriate humor	Uses humor to make for a more relaxed and productive atmosphere	Realizes when and where humor will backfire, and withholds	Uses humor as a uniting dynamic across a range of situations
Can laugh at self and others	Allows others to be funny	Understands that laughter makes a more comfortable meeting, classroom, etc	Recognizing and appreciates a great sense of humor in others

http://www.microsoft.com/education/en-us/Training/Competencies/Pages/humor.aspx

This clearly demonstrates the value of humor in the adult workplace. Indeed, instead of being a distraction to achievement, it can be the very thing that allows it! So how can you help a boy develop his natural affinity for funniness in ways that will help him learn and prepare him to be successful in the world beyond school?

HUMOR FOR LEARNING AT HOME

You probably have much more tolerance for "boy humor" at home. As parents, we innately understand that a boy's sense of humor is a sign of intelligence and often makes us feel good about him. That will not always be the case with a busy teacher in a classroom full of students. Yet your appreciation for his comedy is a great platform from which to teach him how to use his wit in ways that will trigger his learning and keep him out of the principal's office!

Learning with Laughter – Because humor can focus the interest of males, it is a great way to help a boy become interested in a topic or focus on a homework assignment. All it takes is getting him to think about the weird, puzzling, bizarre, or ridiculous aspects of it first. This will draw his attention and get him thinking about your topic. Here are some examples:

- *Finding the funny side* - Say he has an assignment about the solar system. Ask him what funny things would happen if the sun was just a little too close to the earth. This will spur boys on to many foolish assertions, probably including wild ways that people and animals would be fried, burned, etc. Let him have fun with this, but then ask, "Why don't those things happen?" This readies him to think more deeply about the serious topics of distance, balance climate, and the environment. It may also spur him to deepen his knowledge and seek mastery of it. As we shall see, this quest for mastery is a tremendous source of long-term success for boys and it often starts with a joke! The trick is to move from the silly into the serious.

- *Picture this* – Using funny pictures of a topic is another great way to spark a boys' interest in learning as it pairs the two secrets of humor and game. For example, if he has to learn vocabulary for school, start out by asking him to find silly pictures on the internet. Just figuring out the words to use in the search engine will sharpen his understanding of the vocabulary! He may even be able to include them in his report or bring them to share at school—once you have determined with him "where it fits" (more on that below) and the humor tolerance of his teacher (more on that below, too!).

Another fun approach is ask him to draw silly cartoon sketches of each word that someone else has to guess. This requires him to think about how best to represent the essential meaning of the word. His brain will work twice as hard due to the discretionary effort he uses, and he will have deeper, better neural connections that will help him remember and use the vocabulary much better in the future.

To find a neat online tool that uses drawing pictures to help your son learn, go to helpingboyslearn.com and enter H1 in the HBL TIP BOX.

- *Slo-Mo* – This pairs the secrets of movement and humor in a simple way by asking a boy to demonstrate his knowledge by rendering it in slow motion. It is also hilarious. I'm not sure why this is so funny to boys, but it is! Almost anything learned in school can be done this way (science for plant growth, math for explaining place value, language for the stages of a story). For great examples, take a look at the videos on the website! Moving it from silly to serious is as simple as asking him to orally explain or write what happens in his *Slo–Mo.*

For videos of Slo-Mo, go to helpingboyslearn.com and enter H2 in the HBL TIP BOX.

Fighting Fear of Learning – Many boys who struggle in school have moved into "flight" mode because their brains have perceived what happens to be threatening and likely to result in repeated failure and loss of testosterone. However, we also know that humor can be a powerful tool to help males reduce their fear of failure by diminishing the perceived threat and helping them tap the resilience to face challenges. You can use this knowledge at home to prepare your son for success at school.

If you sense that he is apprehensive about learning or has had a bad day at school, using humor to get him to focus on the smallness of the problem in the grand scheme of things is very helpful. With better perspective, he will realize that he does indeed have the ability to handle the problem at hand. Here are a few ideas:

- *Fortunately/Unfortunately* – This old camp game is perfect for taking the stuffing out of a problem. Start by having him state the problem, beginning with, "Unfortunately..."

    o BOY – "Unfortunately I have a test tomorrow that I know I won't do good on..."

Then you can help him make the consequences of the situation more ridiculous and exaggerated. Below is an example:

    o PARENT – "Fortunately, if we study for the next twelve hours solid you'll probably do better!"

    o BOY – "Unfortunately, I have to go to bed at 8:00 o'clock so I can't study that long..."

    o PARENT – "Fortunately, we can just move your bed down here to the kitchen and you can lay in it and study!"

    o BOY – "Unfortunately, you'll fall asleep while we are doing it and I'll escape out of the house so I don't have to study!"

    o PARENT – "Fortunately, I will be able to email all of your teachers to help find you and they will come out in their pajamas to search because they hate it when a boy escapes a test!"

    o BOY – "Unfortunately, the temperature will drop to below -20° and they'll all freeze like statues in their pajamas..."

Continue like this until he starts laughing or has a gleeful look in his eyes...

- *Use **Learning with Laughter** techniques* – Take one of the ideas listed above *(Finding the Funny Side, Picture this, Slo-Mo)* and do it with him to confront the anxiety he has about the learning challenge or task at hand. Again, continue to do it until he is viewing the problem with a better perspective. This may only take a few minutes.

After he is in a better mood, ask a simple question: *"What's the simplest thing you can do to make this problem better?"* Notice that you are not asking him to solve the problem, just to think of something that improves the situation. Resist the parental urge to make a suggestion or solve the problem for him. If he doesn't have any ideas, suggest that you leave the question open, talk about it later, and move on to something else. Be confident of the brain research that demonstrates that once we pose a question that is unanswered about something important, our brains subconsciously work on the problem, trying to come up with an answer while we are thinking about other things. And don't be surprised if he comes up to you later on with an idea for the situation—one that his brain has told him he can put into practice!

Improving His Comedic Timing: Deciding whether it fits –This section is particularly designed for parents who have a son who is always having problems with inappropriate humor or distracting others in school. More than many other forms of communication, humor is "context-situated." In other words, it only really works when it fits into a situation. Simply put, the difference between being seen as a comedic genius or a jerk is all about timing. As adults, we know that what may be appropriate with family members or friends would not be appropriate with the boss at work. Many budding male humorists have not been able to recognize this yet! The problem is that their lack of awareness may create bad reputations at school that prevent them from becoming anything other than a class clown. As will be discussed in later chapters, if a boy feels that his only pathway to significance and meaning is through such clownishness, he will find refuge there, and not develop the other capabilities that he has. This can be avoided by helping him hone his sense of comedic timing. Here are a few ways to do that

- *Why didn't that work?* – Help him to notice when he's trying to be funny and other people aren't laughing. Just saying, "That's not funny" is not enough. He needs to understand why. A great time to do this is after he has had a problem with humor (being disciplined in class or sent to the office, for example). Simply ask him to say why he thought it was funny. Once he responds, ask, "Why do you think your teacher didn't think it was funny?" He might not have any idea, or may say something like, "Because she doesn't have a sense of humor." To get him to understand that it's more than that, review:
    - *What was going on at the time?*
    - *What the teacher and other students were trying to do?*
    - *How she probably felt before and after his humor?*

What you are doing is fostering what I call "stealth empathy." Unlike girls, boys do not release oxytocin when everyone gets along and so feel less compulsion to "read the room" before launching into humor. They are more likely to want the testosterone blast that comes from succeeding at a goal they set for themselves—like making friends laugh. Helping them to imagine what someone else was feeling gives them important understanding that they can use to be a more successful humorist in the future. This is a process, and you may not notice him accepting this, but after a few sessions you should see his approach improve.

- *Connect, don't crush* – Because he likes humor and wants to be successful at it, you can help set your son up for long-term success and reduce any bullying tendencies in his comedy by helping him understand that he will be much more appreciated when his humor connects with people and the common problems that everyone has. Making fun of his own mistakes can endear him to other people because of his faults and not despite them. By using the techniques highlighted earlier which encourage him to laugh at his problems and keep them in perspective can develop this sense of "self-deprecating" humor which communicates strength and security and not insecurity and neediness. When one seeks to "crush" another with humor (i.e. cruel put-downs or making fun of someone different), it just demonstrates that they are afraid. Adults, particularly women, need to be aware that context matters here, too. As we have seen, boys who are friends will razz each other as a sign of connectedness; this is different than singling out another with whom he has no friendship.

- *Highlight different types of humor* – If he loves being funny, you can play into his desire for mastery by introducing him to other types of humor beyond slapstick and silliness. Here are some for him to discover, recognize, and try out in his speaking and writing :

For a list of different types of humor and examples, go to helpingboyslearn.com and enter H3 in the HBL TIP BOX.

o Wry humor

o Wit

o Irony

o Satire

o Repartee

o Self-effacing humor

HUMOR IN THE CLASSROOM

Because humor is such an effective way of leveraging motivated engagement and discretionary effort when used effectively by teachers, I have given them some very clear strategies in the teachers' edition of Helping Boys Learn. Surveys consistently indicate that teachers who have a sense of humor become more significant teachers in the lives of their students.

If you would like to share some powerful ways to use humor to foster learning in class with your son's teacher or principal, download a teacher tip sheet by going to helpingboyslearn.com and enter HT in the HBL TIP BOX.

Boys Learn Through Challenge

A test of skills for a worthy cause

"This stuff's too easy; I could do it if I wanted to. But I don't..."
—Grade 8 student

It was 4 p.m. in the principal's office, and the intervention team was wrapping up their case conference about Tim Sobey and his lack of success in school. Many of the efforts made to engage him in class had been reviewed, and there was a clear air of frustration in the room.

"If only Tim would put more effort into class, I know he would do better," his grade 5 teacher said, sighing. "He doesn't even appear to try sometimes."

"It's not your fault, Mrs. Morris," Tim's mother said to the teacher. "He's just so lazy. I don't know why; his sister has always worked so hard in school."

"She was an easy one, wasn't she?" Ms. Tream, the special education teacher, added. "How is it going in high school?"

"She's on the honor roll," said Tim's mother proudly.

"I remember teaching her," said Mrs. Morris wistfully. "She certainly had great self-discipline and focus."

"And so it doesn't appear that Tim has any of that, hmmm?" said Mr. Thompson, the school principal, almost to himself as he looked out of the window in his office. Tim had been a frequent visitor to his office this year, and Mr. Thompson was very familiar with the perception around school that the boy was a slacker who wouldn't amount to much. Yet he knew from their interactions that Tim was both intelligent and curious. The principal turned back to the group. "You know, I've been watching him out in the parking lot as we've been meeting for the last 45 minutes. He's been on his skateboard, repeating the same thing over and over—I think it's some kind of jump. He certainly has discipline and focus, but he's not choosing to show it in Mrs. Morris's class. Are there other areas where he displays this kind of commitment, Mrs. Sobey?"

After thinking for a moment, Tim's mother responded, "Yes, as a matter of fact he collects these kind of 'action-figure' cards—I don't know what they are. But he spends hours online looking at them, and knows other kids and adults all around the world who do the same thing. It's ridiculous, really. They're just cards, and the ones they really want seem so hard to find. But he keeps at it. He just seems to love the challenge."

Just Lazy?

If your son expresses little interest in working hard at learning in school it can be very frustrating. You work hard to provide for him, and know it's hard to succeed in the "real world" beyond school; he needs to work hard so he doesn't get left behind. The behavior of a boy like this appears to reflect a character issue of selfishness or laziness. The adults give and give, but these guys don't want to give anything back. They can't seem to be bothered. In the classroom or at home they may produce some work if the pressure is on, but their production flags once the pressure is removed—so they accomplish little to nothing. Worse, they are probably not contributing members of the classroom community. They may waste the teacher's time, distract or set bad examples for other students, and rarely contribute positively to class efforts.

The irony of this for parents and teachers is their knowledge that, like Tim, most boys have areas in their lives outside of school where they will put in tremendous effort. They work hard playing sports, engaging in hobbies like computer games and collections, and participating in after-school social groups or part-time jobs that demand a great deal of commitment. Yet in school, that effort seems rationed. Why is this so? Why do they exert effort and commitment in some places, but not others? In this chapter, we will investigate what will leverage long-term commitment to learning. We've seen that boys love to learn with movement, using games, and with humor. We've highlighted why those pathways seem to appeal to the male brain and engage males more deeply in what is being taught. There are other, more profound approaches to explore if we want a boy to claim responsibility for his schoolwork. Challenge, mastery, and meaning are all interconnected in this quest. Let's look first at challenge and find out why a difficult undertaking often seems to bring out the best in boys.

Why challenge helps boys to learn

We know that males are quite capable of focused attention when playing a game. Winning has powerful physiological effects due to the testosterone blast that males receive when they succeed. Studies have shown that males who triumph in highly competitive and challenging games have the highest levels of testosterone. Indeed, just imagining success has been shown to increase testosterone levels in men. Many so-called "alpha males" are frequently unsuccessful in classroom situations as boys. Nevertheless, they receive admiration from others in society and especially from other males. It's easy to see why a boy who is a good hockey player might not see the same benefits coming from working hard in school. He does not naturally experience the same physical "high" or recognition in his peer group from a completed assignment as he does from a goal. Add to this the fact that hockey naturally plays to his brain-wired strengths for movement, and it's easy to imagine that school will always take a back seat to hockey. This becomes a source of despair for parents and teachers because they believe school-based learning will likely be much more beneficial to the boy in 15 years than his hockey skills.

This is where the concept of challenge becomes most important. The challenge of the game and the rewards of winning are motivators for males. It's easy to think that this takes place most often for males in sports or video games, but challenge is actually the basis for male efforts in many areas. Mountain climber George Mallory became famous in the 1920s with his response to a reporter's question, "Why do you want to climb Mount Everest?" He retorted, "Because it is there." In that response he spoke for countless males throughout history who have explored new frontiers, launched enterprises in the face of extreme odds, and engaged in death-defying feats. More darkly, it also evokes the rationale for terrible wars, violence, and destruction unleashed on others. We will examine other aspects of the male ego that might influence the decisions leading to both heroic and dastardly actions later, but it is important to recognize that conquering perceived challenges was a significant goal in all of them.

Challenge works as a learning tool with boys because they crave it and use it to discover things about themselves and their environment. Remember the "ring toss" experiment noted earlier? The task of getting the rings around the post was fairly simple, but the males in the study needed to make it interesting by tossing the rings from challenging distances. In the process, they were no doubt attempting different strategies using speed, spin, and height, with the goal of improving their performance. This unconscious drive for mastery is triggered naturally and without prompting when males decide to respond to a challenge. But there are important aspects of the male approach to challenge that must be kept in mind. These have to do with how a boy perceives the challenge he is facing. To use challenge as a successful tool for motivated engagement and discretionary effort at home and school, it is important to focus on three areas:

- His personal "resources" available
- How the challenge is created
- Its relationship to his personal interests and goals

Let's take a look at each one of these more closely:

Personal resources available to meet the challenge – Adults who try to help boys struggling in school know the frustration of the boy who refuses to attempt a challenge that we know he could complete with a little effort. In terms of schoolwork, however, there may be other forces at work. An 11-year-old boy who has had little success with classroom challenges since he entered school at age five has had many testosterone-based physiological events of failure that tell him that, no matter what adults say, he can't do well in school. One boy expressed this quite honestly and eloquently to his principal, putting it this way: "Sir, when I try in school and don't do well, I feel terrible. But if I don't try much and then don't do well, I don't feel bad. I don't like feeling bad all the time, so I don't try."

In **KEEN For Learning**, I describe the power of neural pathways created in the brain when the learner feels threatened. His amygdala and other evolutionarily processes in his brain are reacting with the fight-or-flight syndrome in the same way they would if he were a primitive hunter being forced to pursue an animal on the Savannah that was clearly impossible to catch or kill. If he fights, it's not going to be against the animal challenging him, it will be against the forces making him endanger his survival by depleting his psychological resources in an improbable effort. His response is to take flight now and save his intensity for attacking an animal (or assignment) that he can slay! One may feel this over-dramatizes the situation, but I have looked into the eyes of these boys and seen the fear and despair that is hidden under their nonchalance and bravado. I know how deeply failure in school impacts their psyche.

The only way to change this perception is through creating a successful progression of learning tasks that indicate to a boy that he can be good at class work and meeting school challenges. Once he believes that, he will be willing to take on other, more complex challenges. Eventually, he will look forward to and seek out ways to demonstrate his abilities. Failing at an attempt in school will deter him no more than striking out would for a good baseball player—it may be disappointing, but lessons can be learned and failure often increases his determination to succeed the next time. It becomes a challenge to be taken on and conquered. But like the famous mountain climber Mallory, a boy will more enthusiastically attempt to scale his own Everest after having repeated successes on other, smaller mountains.

How the challenge is created – Building resilience in male learners to take on learning challenges is best accomplished when:

- *The size of the challenge is appropriate* – The tasks are specifically laid out and have a restricted timeline that has a clear beginning and end. Larger tasks and assignments need to be broken down into specific subtasks that can be accomplished one step at a time.
- *A time frame for the challenge is clearly set* – Once the task has been clearly defined, a boy should be left to accomplish it

within the specified time period. This time frame should be agreed to and adhered to by the boy.

- *There is downtime built in to the schedule before the next challenge* – All tasks should include a period of downtime if the task is accomplished within the specific time frame. If he accomplishes it within the time period, the boy should be allowed to choose a downtime activity before the next task. If he accomplishes it earlier than the assigned time, and still has met the agreed-upon success criteria, he should be allowed whatever extra time has been gained as well.

Over time, the size and length of the challenges can be increased, but these elements will still be important. In the beginning, make sure that the challenge is time-defined and goal-oriented. Remember that for millennia males have developed the ability to intensely focus for defined periods of time. However, this effort uses a lot of cognitive energy that can drain males and could be one reason that male brains at rest have so much less activity going on—they are "recharging" for the next challenge. The image of the caveman staring at the fire after the hunt seems to be a perfect illustration for this. For modern males, this "recharging" can be observed in relaxation activities such as reading the paper, watching TV, playing repetitive video games, aimlessly shooting baskets, kicking a soccer ball, or hanging out in ways that require moderate physical exertion. Whatever it is, knowing that this downtime is coming is crucial to males undertaking challenges.

How the challenge relates to his personal goals/interests – Because he craves and learns from them, a boy is constantly finding challenges to contend with. He is used to doing it, whether it's shooting five baskets in a row, getting to the next level in a video game, learning a new move on the skateboard, finding a new addition to his card collection—or even seeing how long he can bug his sister until she yells.

He is used to setting his own challenges or taking up those he deems interesting. When he is involved in the planning of the challenge, it helps him take ownership and gives him a chance to focus where he has interest. When creating the challenge, it is important to remember that once boys have conquered a challenge, they often look for a new one. It does not make sense to them to have to meet the same challenge over and over again, unless it has a new twist or unless they have decided it is worthwhile to do it.

Challenge and School

Knowing how important challenge is for boys and the fact that they love to create ways to be challenged, it is also clear that a boy who decides that school is not a place of worthy challenge will not put as much effort into classroom activity. They are saving their cognitive energy for challenges outside of school, ones that they know from experience bring tremendous physiological and psychological rewards. Most boys won't consciously understand this, but neither do many parents or teachers! It is even worse when those adults downplay the importance of boys' challenges in sports and games by proclaiming how much more valuable school is than the time they waste on games and pastimes.

This can create a very unfortunate dynamic where a boy meets his need for challenge by seeing how he can "beat" the system—doing as little work as possible, cheating, or constantly distracting and calling attention to himself. Sensing the adults don't care about what's really important to him, he sees no reason why he should cooperate in a place where he's set up to fail. Students can become masters at this game, and mastery is extremely important to boys. When a boy finds that this type of negative behavior gives him a worthy challenge (not to mention admiration from his peers for standing up to authority), it can become extremely difficult for both teachers and parents. Even worse, such a dynamic effectively ends classroom learning for him. As a parent, you may only realize this has been happening when the ominous phone call from school comes, informing you that your son is now a disciplinary problem.

Even if the dark side of male challenge-seeking does not reach this level in class, it's still a problem that none of a boy's self-defined challenges can be met in school. Neither he, his teacher, nor the other students will benefit from the best part of himself—the part that is dedicated to self-improvement and reaching his potential. Instead, he will ration his cognitive energy and effort, releasing it unreliably and in dribs and drabs, frustrating himself, other students, and the adults in his life who are trying to help him.

However, if you understand your son's need for challenge and can help him harness it in support of learning at home and in the classroom, you can help him to direct his energies in better ways. He can become passionately engaged, a leader for others, and a student who reaches unexpected levels of achievement in both school and life! So let's look at few ways to use challenge for learning at home.

Using challenge to help boys learn

Helping boys successfully meet learning challenges outside of school improves their ability to accomplish learning tasks in the classroom. In particular, small "wins" in learning challenges are easy to create and build upon. Let's begin with some ideas that can be used daily outside of school:

CHALLENGE FOR LEARNING AT HOME

1. *Tell me something I don't know* – This is a much more enjoyable and effective version of the kid-dreaded "What did you learn in

school today?" In a friendly competition, each time you play this, a child creates a question from something he learned that day. So if your son discovered that rabbits are born blind, he could ask: "How are rabbits different from people when they are born?" If you do not know the answer, then he tells you and you repeat it. Then it's your turn to ask a question. This can be made into a game where each participant has to ask a new question in addition to one that has already been asked and answered previously!

Research points out that creating questions can help your son think and learn better while becoming passionate about learning! There is no need to restrict the questions to things that are "school-approved," either. For example, a question like "How many levels does it take to get to the master level in the video game *Super Flight*?" is perfectly acceptable. This may not be information that an adult thinks is useful, but the goal is to have the boys take ownership of creating learning challenges, and that will be done best with topics that interest them. When it's your turn, you can focus on topics you think are more important to know.

To see a parent playing this game with her son, go to helpingboyslearn.com and enter C1 in the HBL TIP BOX.

2. *Establish "The Homework Challenge" game* – A more refined version of the **Beat the Clock** game in Chapter 2, application works particularly well if your son is the type who tends to stare at the ceiling and takes two hours to do a 30-minute school assignment, or if he is not really motivated to do it with any attention to quality. The most basic approach is to use a timed challenge. Ask

him to think of how quickly he could do the assignment correctly. Once he answers, add five minutes and set a timer. Tell him he has five minutes extra just in case he can't do it in the time he predicted; you may sound a bit doubtful of his success, if you wish. There aren't many males who wouldn't think, "Oh yeah? You don't think I can do it? Well, I'll show you." If he succeeds within the time frame, congratulate him and let it go at that. In this case, I wouldn't attach a reward to it; if he enthusiastically embraces the challenge, he is receiving his own reward, both physiologically and psychologically. If you find that his estimate is too optimistic, then limit the scope of the challenge to part of the assignment ("Why don't we try it with just the first two questions?"). It is better to build up easy success than trigger a "flight" from the challenge because he knows it's unlikely to be met.

You may be concerned that a boy will rush and produce sloppy work just to get it done. Indeed, this may happen initially. However, by adding quality challenges as you progress (e.g. "I wonder if you can write this paragraph without any spelling mistakes"), then you can progressively improve his quality control. I have seen that when we started with a speed focus—which inherently appeals to boys—we were able to translate that into better overall work in short order. More importantly, it led to more ownership of learning. You may very well find that he starts to challenge himself in this way without prompting. This all plays into a male's need for mastery and meaning in ways that we'll highlight in the next chapter.

3. *Leverage small wins toward greater challenges* – If your son struggles in school, make sure to track the times he demonstrates accomplishment in any area of school learning. When he does succeed, ask him what else he could do like that. Don't make it

an "assignment," just something to think about; remember the research that suggests that males can get a jolt of testosterone by just thinking about meeting challenges. And don't be surprised if he later comments that he has decided to tackle his newly planned challenge.

To download a certificate that can be used by you to recognize a boy's "small wins," go to helpingboyslearn.com and enter C2 in the HBL TIP BOX.

4. *Discover where he admires challenge* – Challenge is everywhere in your son's interests. The sports stars, celebrities, or musicians he likes have all had to meet challenges in order to succeed.. Likewise, the video games boys love create a series of challenges for their players to meet.. Get him to think about this by asking why the athlete is so good or why the game is so much fun. Invariably, you can point out that the pleasure is in the challenges that the sports figure meets, or that the video game makes him navigate challenges before he can win. The transition from popular culture to learning can be done with statements like:

- What (sports figure, music star, video game character) has met the most challenges in his/her career? What types of challenge do you like best?
- When and where was your best challenge at school?
- What things at school are too easy or boring because there's no challenge? How could this be changed?

As the boy begins to share his views on challenge, do not judge his answers or try to direct the discussion. Just listen. This will set the stage for having him take up challenges and attain mastery.

4. *Introduce "unlikely achievers"* – Share with your son the stories of people who met challenges and were successful despite what others thought. Discussion about these types of people can provide models of others like himself who struggled, but then overcame their struggles and fulfilled their potential. The pathways of achievers like Thomas Edison (science), Walt Disney (entertainment), and Stan Smith (sports) can fire the imagination of your son the same way scaling Everest captivated Mallory!

To access a list of unlikely achievers that can inspire your son, go to helpingboyslearn.com and enter C3 in the HBL TIP BOX.

USING CHALLENGE IN THE CLASSROOM

Teachers often make use of challenge, but sometimes they are not as aware of how powerful challenges can be to leverage motivated engagement and discretionary effort from boys. It's a pretty clear indication that the challenge quotient in class needs to be raised if a boy constantly complains about school being "boring." If that happens, you may want to share the resource below with his teacher.

For teacher tip sheet with some practical strategies for embedding challenge in the classroom, go to helpingboyslearn.com and enter CT in the HBL TIP BOX.

SECRET 5
Boys Learn by Mastery
Ownership is the pathway to passion

"You're not the boss of me!"
—Angry grade 1 student to his teacher

Nick was thrilled. He had just learned to read and now the seven-year-old from New England was determined to share his newfound knowledge with everyone he met. His favorite technique for doing this was to read aloud everything he saw, whether it was a book, a sign, or a passing T-shirt. He was in fine form as he accompanied his friend's family on a camping trip to Quebec. As he sat in the back of the car with some of his books, he insisted on sharing every glorious word of the stories with his friend's family. Then he regaled them with passing road signs: "Exit 24!" "Farm Equipment for Sale!" "Bridge to Canada five miles!"

Needless to say, this was exhausting for both Nick and the other travelers in the car. Finally, during the long wait to cross the border, he fell asleep. The adults in the front seat exchanged relieved glances. Later, as the car sped through Quebec toward the campground, Nick awoke. Refreshed, he set about looking for signs to read. He tried a number of times but could only choke out parts of words. He burst into tears and got so upset his friend's parents pulled the car over.

"What's wrong?" they asked.

"I've forgotten how to read!" he wailed inconsolably.

His friend's parents eventually calmed him down, and while suppressing smiles, they explained that he had not forgotten "how" to read, he just didn't understand French and that's why he couldn't read the signs. Apparently relieved, he then returned to his cheerful self and enjoyed the rest of the vacation. The adults noted, however, that for the remainder of the trip—despite repeated promptings—he refused to read anything out loud, even the books he had brought with him that he knew by heart.

This story, taken from an anecdote told by literacy researcher Jeffrey Wilhelm, is an excellent example of the male need for mastery and its profound influence on how boys approach learning. There is something about mastery that satisfies deep longing in the male psyche. As we shall see, this need often manifests itself in unexpected ways, but once you start looking for it, you can see it in many different places, including in the lives of underachieving boys at home and school.

In school, mastery applied to learning is success with assignments and tests; if a boy is not interested in mastering these things, he might be labeled a "slacker." Even worse, he may be seen as a distraction to learning who does as little as possible while preventing classmates from attaining their own level of mastery. There are many reasons for this perception. Boys often do not ask teachers for help when they are having problems with class work. Unlike girls, they often avoid using the expertise of the teacher to help them achieve. Indeed, boys may have little need to affiliate with or please the teacher. In many situations, there is social ostracism from male peers for any boy who is seen to be "sucking up" to the teacher by caring too much about classwork. If they accomplish in school, boys seem to want to do it by themselves, even if that approach is more difficult.

Yet, when we observe boys doing what they love—even if they are unsuccessful in school—it becomes clear that mastery is very important to them. Mastering an intricate skateboard maneuver, getting to the highest level in a video game, or being the best in a sports competition are things on which boys will spend an incredible amount of discretionary effort. This includes boys who have been "identified" with attention deficits or learning disabilities. The question is, why don't they strive for it more in the classroom? Before we can answer that, we need to understand better what it is about mastery that makes it so powerful for males.

Why pursuit of mastery helps boys learn

A reflection upon mastery in the context of boys' learning must consider the four "secrets" revealed earlier: action, game, humor, and challenge. Because of their strong appeal to the way the male brain is wired, these four pathways to learning are very powerful. They immediately engage and motivate boys. But their effectiveness is highest in the moment and does not necessarily help boys become self-motivated, passionate learners who can sustain a commitment to learning over a long period of time. That is why mastery is so important; it encourages a boy to repeatedly apply discretionary effort in the service of self-improvement. It is the secret that helps boys move beyond their evolutionary physiology and toward their true potential in our modern world.

Characteristics of mastery

We have seen that movement and games are extremely powerful for the male brain. Much of the game-based movement that attracts boys requires a high level of precise accuracy in bodily/kinesthetic movement or the manipulation of objects in space. Whether it is placing the object in the net (soccer, hockey, basketball), maneuvering around other cars at high speeds (Nascar), hitting a ball with a stick (golf, baseball, tennis), or accruing points by firing at rapidly moving aliens across a screen (video games), controlled movement is the key element. For boys, winning the game and receiving the pleasurable "testosterone blast" that accompanies success is directly related to how well the skills for the game are mastered. Let's examine the characteristics of mastery that can be helpful in using it to help boys learn:

1. **The pathway and value of mastery is clear and evident** – There is a logical and close cause and effect relationship that shows boys what must be done to achieve mastery. This is obvious in sports: If you have succeeded in putting the ball in the net, no one has to explain it—it is clear for all to see.

2. **It demonstrates individual control applied in a social context** – A boy may play these games with others, but he often spends a great deal of time preparing for the game and practicing the skills alone. The social aspect of the game is secondary to the skill aspect in a way it is not for most girls. That is because the boy must feel personal control over what he is doing to become invested in it. Extremely strong social bonds can be formed between boys in games, but usually only after their skills have been tested together and the level of mastery for each boy has been revealed.

3. **It needs to be tested and publicly demonstrated** – It is only through the challenge of measuring one's skills against an opponent or standard of excellence that the value of those skills is recognized by most boys. The public demonstration of improved levels of mastery validates for them that the effort expended in achieving it has been worthwhile.

4. **Coaching is most effective *after* failure** – When a boy wants to develop mastery of something but has not been successful, he is much more likely to allow someone else to teach him than before he has experienced failure. This works best in a coaching context where the coach stands alongside the boy and helps him achieve a higher level of mastery through focused and targeted interventions designed specifically to improve his skills and enhance future success.

5. **Basic mastery precedes the desire to reach higher** – We have seen that the male brain tends to avoid challenges that it perceives as too difficult at first glance. However, after small successes, the need for challenge spurs boys to seek out more difficult challenges. Crucial to this is a basic mastery of certain skills that boys have learned and can demonstrate to themselves and others. Specific challenges are often sought precisely because they can help boys develop and demonstrate competence in areas that are important to them.

Even boys' approach to humor can be seen from the perspective of mastery, particularly the humor that illustrates a power reversal where those in authority are shown to have the same flaws and foibles as everyone else. This equalizing power of humor allows boys to verbally claim mastery over others when it does not exist in reality. This type of approach comes from a place of fear and allows males to maintain forward momentum when faced with challenges by those in authority. Another area of humorous mastery for boys involves the use of sly "inside jokes" and understated turns of phrase that demonstrate skill in finding humor in any situation and expressing it subtly.

"What's it good for?"

For males, underlying the desire for mastery is a need for control. But why does the male ego seem to need to control objects, circumstances, and, indeed, people? And how is this relevant in a school classroom? I believe these questions lead us to one of the core differences between the male and female brain, and one of the greatest misunderstandings and frustrations for parents and teachers trying to help boys learn.

When confronted with the same situation, boys and girls will ask different questions about it. For girls, the question tends to be "What's it like?" They seek to understand the qualities of a person, place, or thing so that they can understand how to relate to it. Boys, on the other hand, ask "What's it good for?" They want to understand how to use it and what effects they can create with it. Ask a young boy to talk about an object and he will focus most intensely on what it does and how you can use it. A young girl is much more likely to describe what she is interested in by describing its characteristics and how it fits into a social situation.

Gender researcher Leonard Sax ascribes these differences to neural wiring. Girls' hearing and eyesight are much better attuned to observing finer details and discriminating minor differences. The fact that their brains naturally wire more intensely for oral language means that they can put their observations into words. They have a larger descriptive vocabulary than boys for things like color, because they can see a wider spectrum. That's why you will rarely hear a boy describe his shirt as "teal" or "lime"—he's lucky if he can identify "green."

So what does this have to do with mastery? Girls' ability to notice details and the wide array of characteristics in any situation coupled with their tendency to link these things to social interaction means that "mastery" in these areas would be nearly impossible. Because the social landscape is ever-shifting, it is easier to work collaboratively with frequent feedback from others to understand how everything fits together. and not as attractive or easily attained. This is borne out in the research indicating that in school, girls achieve higher but are harder on themselves—they do not believe they are as good as their grades indicate. The teacher's feedback is thus important for girls to know whether they are succeeding and fitting in well into the social structure of the classroom. On the other hand, boys often achieve lower but believe they are smarter! They don't see success as related to classroom social structure—unless it is useful to them in some way.

The root of this male need for usefulness can also be found in the past. Over millennia in hunter/gatherer societies, male brains evolved to pay close attention to the usefulness of people, places, and things in the struggle to survive. Large social groups were not of value unless everyone had a specific role and contribution to make. Males developed their skills as hunter before they were allowed to hunt, often after going through a long apprenticeship to make sure that they could contribute to the hunt when the time came. As societies evolved from agricultural to industrial, so did this practice, but the value of skill mastery for practical applications was always present, whether in the guilds of the Middle Ages or the farmers and factory workers of the 20th century. Schools have always had a mandate to support the development of these practical skills and have often used "vocational" education for this purpose. However, until recently, males often left school early and apprenticed on the farm, factory, or workplace. This approach made male learning "useful" for society. Interestingly enough, the standardized testing found in schools today evolved in an effort to assess the usefulness of the learning that occurs in classrooms.

The legacy of useful male learning affects a modern boy's approach to school in three ways:

1. **It's only worthwhile if it "counts"** – Teachers have tried to show the utility of learning by marks. The students' refrain of "Does this count on the test?" or "Are we being marked on

this?" is an illustration of this type of male approach to learning, as is the title of Jeffrey Wilhelm's book on male literacy: *Reading Don't Fix No Chevys*. For boys to put discretionary effort into something, it must count and have a tangible result. This orientation is also seen in the male desire to count and record data related to games. We have already discussed how movement and challenge draw males to sports games, but an equally powerful attraction is the numbers and statistics that are represented by things like baseball's ERA (Earned Run Average). Very few girls are interested in collecting information of this sort, but as a school principal I routinely met boys who could recount a year's worth of scoring statistics of their favorite team while finding it seemingly impossible to remember a few simple answers for a social studies test that day. For many males, it seems that these statistics make achievement more "real." It is clear that boys prize a "just the facts" approach to many areas of learning and that mastery of these facts is worthy of effort. An example of this on a global scale is Wikipedia, where a whopping 85% of those who contribute facts are male.

2. **Structure is the pathway to mastery** – The fascination for facts and their ordering points to deeper needs for boys as they search for mastery: structure and organization. One of the reasons that facts and statistics are comforting is that they serve as useful tools in confronting the chaos of the universe. They allow a sense of control. This is increased when boys create structures clearly identifying the order and function of each part, as well as a "pecking order" clarifying the relationship between the parts.

Males often apply this to social relationships, needing to know where they stand in relation to others. Extreme examples are found in the structure of every army that has been formed throughout history. Designed by males, these organizations have very strict orders of rank and function and strict sanctions for anyone who does not "fall in line." But there are seen wherever boys come together in groups. When there is no predefined structure, the boys create a pecking order, usually based on physical ability and strength. When the order is not clear, conflict is often seen as a useful way to clarify it. In school, I observed that physical fights between boys were often the precursors to a deeper social relationship and even friendship between boys, since they clarified the nature of that relationship. Contrarily, in almost all cases, physical conflict between girls ruined the possibility of a future friendship.

Completion is Important – Structure and organization also serve an important role for males because they highlight the certainty of task completion. If primitive hunters did not complete their task of finding and slaying food, they starved. The male brain evolved to help males be extremely focused and energized when completing tasks like this. However, since this caused a huge expenditure in cognitive and physical energy, males also developed tendencies to reserve their energy for those things that made evolutionary sense such as physical safety, pursuit of food, and procreation. Working efficiently in groups with structure and role division meant that the energy expenditure could be reduced even further, but only if each participant's "skill mastery" was assured. Games were well-suited to this purpose, and there are still many games that males enjoy today that have the characteristics of the hunt: players striving to reach defined goals and filling defined roles, usually within a limited time frame.

This evolutionary legacy makes many boys loathe to expend energy on work that seems to have little or no practical purpose, since the mastery of such work seems pointless. This is a major problem that parents and teachers face with a boy who does not achieve in school. Happily, however, we can tap into the male desire for mastery to provide the solution to this problem, which is found in helping boys experience the unparalleled satisfaction of controlling the only real thing they have control over: themselves.

The ultimate goal: self-mastery

The boy who told his teacher she wasn't "the boss" of him was making it clear that he wanted no part of what was going on in the classroom at that moment. Instead, he wanted to do what he wanted to do and that was it. And for many, particularly women, that's the problem with males in a nutshell: the essentially ego-driven selfishness and need to be the "boss" that has caused so many problems in our world. We have seen that there is an evolutionary element in this that caused female brains to wire in a way that sought social cohesion and accommodation with others while male brains prompted them to more physical aggression and independent action. Yet society has consistently evolved to moderate the extremes of the male brain, channeling the anti-social elements into socially acceptable forms. All major religious faiths have injunctions and rituals to accomplish the same thing. As I argued in the first chapter, however, the modern world has put males at a crossroads: to go forward successfully they will need to consciously choose to exhibit the best aspects of their neural wiring (goal-setting, intense focus, courageous risk-taking, etc.) in ways that will serve them today.

It is precisely at this juncture where the phrase "you're not the boss of me" becomes a deeper and more profound statement that points to a better way for boys in both school and life. Who is the "boss" of you? In the end, of course, it is you. Despite all of the constraints that we may have as individuals in North American society, even the poorest of us have more economic and personal freedom than the vast majority of humans who ever lived before us. And our greatest freedom is our ability to make decisions and take actions that affect our lives. The success of these actions is not guaranteed, but there is little doubt that the qualities that come with self-mastery (self-discipline, commitment, emotion moderation, and persistence, among others) make up the foundation for both success and satisfaction in most situations in life. Children with skills in self-mastery do not become the ones who are in trouble at school, failing on their report cards, or dropping out of school. Recent research has indicated that tendencies toward self-mastery (self-regulation) can be seen in children as young as four years old, and that children with those tendencies fare better in every way, both in school and throughout life. Because of this, some argue that little can be done at home or school after this age, but I believe there are good ways for parents and teachers to foster self-mastery in their boys on a daily basis.

Mastery and School

Before discussing ways to foster self-mastery, let's look briefly at what can happen in school when a boy's need for mastery is misdirected. If a boy struggles with learning in school or is disengaged and underachieving, his need for mastery often enters the fight-or-flight mode. In fight mode he seeks power; in flight mode he looks outside the classroom. Neither is a good option.

The struggle for power

If you are a parent who has an underachieving boy on your hands, I don't need to describe to you the variety of ways he can turn a learning situation into a power struggle. You may be dealing with it daily! Maybe he's never said "You're not the boss of me" out loud, but by doing any of the following he can send that message loud and clear:

- Disrupting the class with his inappropriate remarks or attempts at humor
- Calling out while you or others are talking
- Making snide or cutting remarks out loud or under his breath
- Refusing to complete work
- Completing work, but with as little effort as possible
- Wanting to have the last word in a discussion
- Blaming you for his lack of effort and/or success
- Trying to spread dissent by engaging others in discussions about an adult's unfairness and unreasonableness

And these behaviors are only the ones that he's consciously displaying!

Much of this behavior can be done unconsciously. Women everywhere seem to share the frustration of male command and control tendencies in relationships where they have to adjust or fix things that were fine already. It's as if nothing can be complete without their male imprimatur. When challenged on this, men will usually deny they were trying to control things and, sometimes with genuine bafflement, say they were just trying to make things better! But the fact remains that seldom do you give a task to a male that doesn't come back morphed with his physical or metaphorical fingerprints on it. As one teacher put it, describing a boy who was actually doing well in her class, "That boy never gives me anything back in the way that I asked for it. He seems to take pride in making small changes that were not asked for or wanted—just to prove he can do it!"

Searching for mastery outside of the classroom

The "flight" response involves mentally checking out of the classroom and searching for mastery elsewhere. Such boys put all of their efforts into things like sports, hobbies, video games and being popular with their peers. They see a pathway to mastery much more clearly in these contexts. In school, they can become "shadow students," who are present in class, but their efforts and achievement are not. They may pretend to be busy with work, but when a teacher or parent looks for it, there's not much there. They frequently have excuses for the lack of production, but these are, in reality, just delaying tactics or feints they use to avoid the situation—or stretch it out until the adults give up or are distracted elsewhere. These boys can often be very pleasant students who are liked by the teacher and recognized in school for their prowess in sports or for other reasons, but they fly under the radar academically, feed off other students in work groups, and are a general drag on the learning of the class community. This all ends badly later when they inevitably find they haven't developed the skills to achieve when they want to in higher learning or a competitive work environment that requires well-developed learning skills.

If a boy is either searching for mastery in the classroom through power struggles or searching for it elsewhere and ignoring the classroom, his success depends on avoiding the fight-or-flight response that males have always used when they feel threatened. How can we help a boy use his need for mastery in the service of learning?

Using mastery to help boys learn

MASTERY AT HOME

There are various ways to help a boy foster self-mastery. In particular, we want to set up situations in which mastery is understood and rewarded within a learning context. However, because this is a deeper process than just engaging him with movement, a step-by-step approach is needed. It involves four stages:

1. Help him think about mastery in his interests
2. Foster mastery with his interests
3. Develop his mastery with your interests
4. Support him achieving mastery at school

Help him think about mastery in his interests – A boy will most often seek mastery in an area where he has a natural interest.. Your focus should be to help him reflect on mastery as a process. As a parent, you can start by recognizing an interest and skill he has— "Wow, you're really good at that video game!"—but then you need to go beyond that. You want to engage him in a conversation about how one achieves mastery. The following questions can be helpful:

- How did you get good at _____?
- What things do you have to be good at (or to win)?
- How do you know you're winning (getting better)?
- What will you have to do to get even better than you are now?
- When do you think you'll get to the next level?

As you discuss this with him, repeat back to him (rephrase) what he is telling you. For example, let's say you're talking about his love of baseball and you've asked him about the things you need to be good at. He tells you that you have to be able to run quickly to catch the ball. You can rephrase it by saying, "So you're good at running fast to the ball when you play baseball?" Continue the conversation with questions like those above, which get him to think about how skilled he is and what else he may need to do to get better. These chats should not be inquisitions! They are just friendly, easygoing interactions that should be repeated with his different areas of interest. They should happen on an ongoing basis as you notice what he likes to do. They may not seem to amount to much on their own,

To watch a video of a parent and son having a conversation like this, go to helpingboyslearn.com and enter MAS1 in the HBL TIP BOX.

but you are helping his brain create neural pathways that deepen his understanding of how to attain mastery.

Foster mastery with his interests – Once you have had some of these conversations with him, you are ready to start helping him achieve mastery and experience the process of self-improvement with conscious growth. It starts by identifying one skill he wants to improve. Your earlier chats would have revealed exactly what one might be best, because he would have admitted that he needed to get better at it. To make sure you've got the right one to start with, challenge him to see if he can improve this skill and tell him you want to help him to do it. His response to this challenge and your offer will tell you if it's the right skill. If it is important to him, his ready acceptance of the challenge indicates his motivated engagement. He may be dubious about your ability to help him (i.e., "C'mon mom, you don't know anything about my video games!"). But you don't need to. Your role will be to provide a structure for his achievement. So tell him you know he's the expert, but you are going to make it easy for him. He'll like that.

Tell him you are going to set up a simple plan. Based on five "Whats," it is called a 5W Plan:

The 5W Plan for Mastery

1. *What specifically does success look like?* Help him pick something achievable that you think he could do with practice. If he has a big goal, break it down into levels and have the plan target the first level. Make it measurable and specific, like catching five ground balls in a row.

2. *What strategies will help him achieve it?* Pick no more than three. He needs to choose them. They can be based on suggestions from you or others, preferably those who have expertise. For example, to improve ground ball catching, his baseball coach might offer some good strategies. When identifying the strategies, remember that those with movement, game, humor, and challenge are most likely to work best!

3. *What is the timeline?* For early 5W Plans to get the best discretionary effort, the timeline should be clear and close. For a preschool boy, one to two days; for an older boy, a week to start. This is the first 5W Plan and the goal is to have a "win" in a boy's first structured effort at conscious growth.

4. *What "mastery checks" will there be?* Like mileposts on the road, these are specific indicators that let you and your son know he is on track to reach his goal. Boys' brains respond well to this approach. It sends the message that learning is a boy's responsibility and can be done without either nagging or coddling. A mastery check can be as simple as a check list that is completed after he has reached certain stages of the task; it shows what he has accomplished thus far. If he has met the criteria for success at that stage, give him a visual cue such as a checkmark. It is even more

powerful if this check is placed on a poster or recorded in another public way.

5. **What** happens after? It is important for a boy's effort to count and be counted. This section of the plan makes it clear how the results of the boy's efforts will be recognized. Examples of recognition should be varied, based on the boy and the specific skill to be mastered. A few examples are:

- *A note on the calendar, picture on the fridge, entry in a "mastery record book"*
- *A certificate of achievement*
- *Telling other people in person, by phone, or online*
- *A related reward provided by a parent*

It's important to recognize that the self-satisfaction that the boy achieves from completing this process is the real reward. This step in the plan is more about reinforcing that satisfaction by formally recognizing the achievement.

To download a 5W Mastery Plan Sheet for use with his interests, go to helpingboyslearn.com and enter MAS2 in the HBL TIP BOX.

Develop his mastery in your interests – Once you have used the 5W Plan as described above, it is time to help him see the value of developing mastery in areas other people think are important. This is an important part of the process that will set the stage for him to work toward mastery in school, but it has the added benefit of making a parent's life easier by reducing stress at home!

To start, just pick something that he is supposed to be doing at home that you have to nag or constantly fight with him about completing (keeping his room clean, making his bed, or feeding the dog, for example). Once you have identified the area for improvement, tell him that because he is so good at using the 5W Plan, you want to use it to make things better for the family—and help him get some things he wants! You then use the plan as outlined above with the following adjustments:

1. **What** *specifically does success look like?* Keep it simple, being specific without overwhelming him. Use the "Rule of Three" if possible. For example, if it's cleaning the room for a seven-year-old, it could be:

- No clothes on the floor
- Bed made
- All toys in toy bin

2. **What** *strategies will help him achieve it?* It is best if he identifies these in a brainstorming session with you. Are there those that can use the secrets of movement, game, and humor to meet this challenge? For example, is there a funny picture he could draw and post on his door or have pop up on the computer screen to remind him?

3. **What** *is the timeline?* When does it need to be done? Every day when he goes to school? Once a week? You decide together.

To see a sample of a boy's completed 5W Mastery Plan for a household chore, go to helpingboyslearn.com and enter MAS3 in the HBL TIP BOX.

4. **What** *"mastery checks"* will there be? A checklist would work here, as long as he completes it and you can follow it.

5. **What** *happens after?* What is the reward for mastering this task? How often is it awarded? How will success be shared with others?

Support him achieving mastery at school – What can a parent do at home to help a boy use this secret to succeed better in school? There are many ways that teachers can foster a boy's desire for mastery to improve learning in the classroom. As in early chapters, a teacher tip sheet is available. But because of the level of discretionary effort that is needed on the boy's part, it really falls to you to be in a supportive coaching role. You will be well-situated to do this if you have experienced with him the first three stages described in this chapter for learning mastery (thinking about it, applying it to his interests, and applying it to your interests). His successful 5W plans are clear evidence of his ability to achieve mastery in both the things that he loves and the things that are important.

To help build on his success at home, the following strategies can help improve his performance at school:

- *Target his favorite subjects* – Just as you began at home with his natural interests, try and begin the mastery focus at school in an area that he already does well in—whether it's math, language, or art. The only criteria is that it's a subject on his report card. Talk with him about setting up a 5W challenge in that subject with some work he already has to do. The 5W plan could be very simple, used for one night and targeted at achieving mastery in a homework assignment. In the span of an hour, you could create a quick plan for it with the 5 W's described above, allow him to complete the assignment correctly and then receive his reward when it's finished! Try it and see if he doesn't find it a fun way to do homework.

- *Report card challenges* – You can use the 5W plan for longer-term situations like report cards. However, this will probably require a number of specific "mastery checks" to make sure he's on track. It may also be necessary to have a number of 5W plans around major projects. Your son will have to identify which ones they should be applied to. Notice the difference between this approach and one in which a parent simply says, "If you get four A's, I'll give you _____." In that situation, everything is left up to the boy. If he struggles at school already, it's almost guaranteed to fail and have the opposite effect than was intended. With the HBL approach, he is building on skills he developed at home, he has a structured plan to follow that makes him consider exactly what it will take to get better grades, and he knows from experience that by following the plan he has a greater chance of success. He becomes "the boss of him" in a real and tangible way.

- *Meet with his teacher* – As a teacher, I was always grateful when a parent showed enough engagement to share with me ways to help her child. If you have used a 5W plan with your child, I would encourage you to make an appointment to help the teacher understand better how to encourage his mastery. It's important to understand how to do this for best effect, though. Few parents comprehend the complexity of teaching a classroom full of children of varying abilities and temperaments who are all required to meet rigorous curriculum standards. You are not an expert in their job or the field of education. But you are an expert on your child. You see the whole of him and know things that his teachers will never know—unless you tell them. Even better, in sharing what you have learned about fostering mastery in your son, you are going to be helping the teacher reach all of the boys in the class! That's the kind of educational leverage teachers are interested in.

When you visit the teacher, talk about how you have used the HBL 5W Plan process to help him seek mastery at home. Give the teacher the tip sheet you have downloaded from the website, and say you are hoping to work with the school to foster his desire to achieve mastery with school work. This is a good time to confirm what school subjects your son has a natural passion and ability in and brainstorm ways to help him apply the 5W process to his daily work. Bringing your son into the meeting may be useful. He will enjoy hearing the description of the 5W Plan successes and be encouraged to work with the teacher to help him do the same at school. A meeting like this is often a breath of fresh air to for everyone involved—especially if your son has struggled in school. This meeting is all about good news, success, and optimism going forward. It builds rapport between you and the school, and I'll let you in on a little "teacher secret" that I know from years in school: The positive, solution-focused way that you have approached this meeting guarantees that your son will get more and better attention from the teacher in the future!

- Let him join an extra-curricular activity that fosters mastery – Research indicates that children who engage in mastery-based activities outside of school actually perform better in class and are more likely to have long term success in school. Activities such as the following teach boys a structured approach to mastery:
    - o Music lessons
    - o Karate or other martial arts
    - o Drama/dance/gymnastics classes
    - o Scouting, cadets
    - o Chess club

- *Set up a mastery group at home* – Mastery groups are very effective when used by teachers in school. The home version involves having your son invite other classmates to make a 5W Plan for something they're studying at school. The focus, however, is not just to get the homework and assignments done that are part of the regular school work, but to go beyond that, finding interesting aspects and real-world applications of what they're studying so that they actually develop expertise beyond what others their age know—perhaps even learning more than the teacher knows about a particular topic. This uses boys' love of game and challenge to help them attain the mastery they seek with school-based topics. Most teachers I know would be happy to let students who did this present their findings to the class and show off their expertise!

MASTERY IN THE CLASSROOM

For teacher tip sheets with some practical strategies for embedding mastery in class, go to helpingboyslearn.com and enter MAST in the HBL TIP BOX.

Boys Learn for Meaning

What is it good for? What am I good for?

*"HOMER: Marge, I'm confused. Is this a happy ending or a sad ending?
MARGE: It's an ending. That's enough."*

—From the television comedy,
The Simpsons

"Dinner is in a few minutes!"

"Mm..." came the distracted response from Aaron-Rey's room. His mother, Tabitha, glanced in. Her 8-year-old was lying on the floor again immersed in an array of toy vehicles, wooden blocks, action figures, and even kitchen utensils he had pilfered from downstairs. She knew that somehow they were all connected in some imaginary world he had created, and he would become very upset if she inadvertently moved any out of place (though it was perfectly all right for *him* to smash them together or throw them around the room, according to the drama he was creating!). She smiled at him and turned to leave.

"Mom, why do I have to go to school?" he asked without looking up.

Tabitha stopped and took a deep breath. She thought they were past this. She felt that he had finally settled into school after the first few years of crying jags, "inappropriate" classroom behavior, meetings with the teachers and principal, and low academic performance. He

[105]

had been such a curious, active, and self-confident little guy before he started kindergarten, but every year since, he seemed to have less and less belief in himself.

"Because it's important," she said. "It's where you learn the things you need when you grow up."

"But I could learn lots here. I could just look on the Internet."

"But what about your friends? You wouldn't see them."

"I can see them lots after school."

"And I'm sure Ms. Orsio would miss you."

"No she wouldn't!" he said vehemently. "She'd be happy if I wasn't there."

"That's ridiculous," Tabitha said, noticing his body tense. She entered her son's room and crouched down beside him, careful not to displace any of the items surrounding him. "I met her at parents' night last week, and she said she was delighted you were in her class."

"She thinks I'm dumb."

"I'm sure she never said anything of the sort."

"She doesn't have to say anything—I know! I see the way she acts toward Sasha, Brittany, and Ahmed. They're the smart ones who can do everything. They get all the smart kid work and I get all the stupid stuff!" His voice was breaking and she knew he'd be in tears in a moment.

Tabitha rubbed her son's back gently. "We talked about this, little man, didn't we? Everyone learns differently and that's not dumb. You and I know how smart you are. Don't worry about doing different work. It's to help you show how smart you really are."

"I know. It's not so much that, it's..." He paused and she could see him struggling for the words that had always come with difficulty to him. "...that I don't *fit*."

With a quick, violent movement that startled her, he swept his arm through the toys, sending them flying across the floor. He turned and looked desperately at her, tears streaming down his face, with a look of anguish that made her chest tighten.

"Why don't I *fit*, Mom? Why?!"

Then he was in her arms, sobbing. As tears welled in her own eyes, she could find no answer for him.

What does it mean?

In a study asking boys why they dropped out of school, their most frequent response was, "It didn't matter. No one cared anyway." We know this is untrue in reality. Schools are filled with people who do care and have dedicated their lives to helping students learn, not to mention the caring of family and friends. It does matter if you finish school, and everyone from parents to politicians say so constantly. Even the dropouts in the study admitted that finishing and achieving highly in school was a good thing. So why say it didn't matter? After working with boys for so many years, my own belief is that those boys were saying, for them, school did not offer a way to build meaning and significance in their lives. They could not see how school would help them personally find their place in the world, either immediately or in the future. When meaning is embedded in the school experience, however, everything changes.

As a teacher, I saw first-hand boys who made amazing transformations. One in particular was named Jeff. For the first three years of high school, he did little work, cut classes, failed courses, got in fights, grudgingly attended summer school, and was on track to drop out. But in his last year, everything changed. He was present at school all the time, he stayed after to ask for help, and his formerly blank stares in class were replaced with a fire in his eyes as he moved to the top of his class in achievement. He approached school like a man on a mission, and it turned out that he was.

During the previous summer, Jeff had been given the opportunity to ride with his cousin, an Emergency Medical Specialist (EMS). He was thrilled by the fast-paced, technical, and high-stakes situations that the ambulance crew dealt with on a daily basis. When he asked how to become one, he was told that he had to graduate high school with good math and science marks and take four more years of college and on-the-job training. He returned to school with a new belief: School mattered for him and he knew exactly why. When I commented on his new-found passion and asked if he liked school better now, he replied, "No, I still hate it. But I can get through it to do what I want." When I told him he sounded just like the philosopher Friedrich Nietzsche, who said, "He who has a why can endure any how," he smiled at me wryly and said, "I'm not one of those smart guys. School just means more now, you know?"

Jeff was able to find meaning in school through a fluke experience and so he was lucky enough to have picked up enough skills during his previous years that he was able to pursue his dreams and eventually become an EMS. But it could have just as easily turned out another way. What if his previous lack of engagement had caused him to miss too much school and his repeated lack of success over 12 years had planted in his mind the belief that no matter how desirable his dream, he just wasn't smart enough to do it? Like Aaron-Rey, all boys need the classroom to help them build meaning and show them where they fit at every stage of their educational experience.

Why meaning helps boys learn

We know that everyone needs meaning in his or her life and that the search for meaning is not a gender-specific endeavor. But, as illustrated by Marge and Homer in the opening quote of the chapter, males and females can find meaning differently. Homer's question expresses the male need for completion, and I'm tempted to think that, for him, Marge's answer was not enough. In the same way that boys and girls can have different tendencies when approaching movement, humor, challenge, and mastery, a boy's approach to meaning tends to be different because of the power inherent in the other places where he goes to learn. The core question that boys have about objects—*"What is it good for?"*—is easily translated to *"What am I good for?"* In the same way that boys use objects in pursuit of their goals, finding meaning by making themselves "useful" is the ultimate satisfaction for males. Another word for that is service. When males use their talents and skills to contribute to their family, team, workplace, community, or society at large, it is a source of tremendous meaning for them and a boon to those with whom they interact.

Boys' ability to influence the world around them in service gives them meaning and becomes a great motivator for males, encouraging them to put both long- and short-term discretionary effort into achieving success in both school and life. Most people would call this ambition. Boys who fail in school are often accused of lacking ambition, but there can be no ambition without meaning. This meaning creates the motivated engagement that pushes boys to stay connected and involved in the world around them and adjusting their efforts and behavior based on the feedback they receive. But why is meaning so important?

The need for greatness

Every young boy wants to be a hero. This theme is universal, manifesting in the myths and fables of ancient times, as well as popular male culture—the celebrities in sports, business, and movies. But a boy chooses a hero because he does something. Those feats of skill and talent confirm to the boy that greatness is possible, and make him reflect on how he could attain it. The need for personal greatness is possibly part of the male evolutionary heritage, where the actual accomplishment in the hunt was the difference between life and death, and those who demonstrated superior accomplishments were held in esteem by the tribe. Whatever its specific origin, it is still a part of the male psyche.

The repercussions of this need have been a double-edged sword. In terms of negative consequences, the damage and misery that the male ego is capable of inflicting upon humanity does not need detailing here. Suffice it to say that for every large historic example of inflated ego and megalomania like Adolf Hitler, there are many "little Hitlers" whose influence, although smaller, is just as destructive in their many spheres of social interaction. They find their significance in mastery and manipulation of others. They are "legends in their own minds" who strive to constantly protect their egos from any outside threat to their greatness. Yet, this has not been true of those who have used their need for greatness to produce goodness in business, education, medicine, and the arts, and it is not true of males who become heroes in daily life, making quiet but significant contributions to their families and communities. These are people to whom the phrase "he's a great guy" genuinely applies.

We have a powerful opportunity to help engender more of these "great guys" by helping boys integrate their need for greatness into learning and school. As a parent, you can help your son see the pathways and rewards of service, allowing him to experience meaningful forms of greatness that are beneficial to himself and others. The most effective way to accomplish this is, again, to start with those places where boys most naturally learn and use the resulting achievement and personal satisfaction to help them understand the value of contributions within a community.

Teamwork and Meaning

Helping a boy develop the skills to work well in a team is key to reconciling his egotistical heroic impulses and his need to fit in and be good for something. When boys are working together with others, contributing their effort and talents and allowing others to share theirs, learning is much more enjoyable and effective for everyone involved. Teamwork is key in helping boys understand how working with a group is advantageous in helping them reach their goals. But boys and girls approach working together differently, and boys will not find meaning when they are simply put in a group situation and told to "cooperate."

The difference between how male and female brains experience being together is important to understand. When girls are placed in a situation where a group works well together, studies have shown that their brains release the powerful hormonal neurotransmitter oxytocin, also called the "tend and befriend" chemical. This causes girls to more easily sublimate their ego to the needs of the group—or at least appear to do so. A significant part of the meaning that girls receive from working together is found in the act of being together. This is not the case with most boys. With their higher levels of testosterone, being together is only relevant if they can do something together. When that something is not worthy, clearly defined, or achievable in boys' eyes, then group work becomes an opportunity to shut down, sponge off others, goof off, play games, or, perhaps most problematic, attempt to assert egotistic mastery within the group. But when there is a challenge that must be overcome, a difficult problem to solve, or some pathway to glory available that can only be attained by joint action, boys will voluntarily sublimate their egos and find meaning in the selfless service to the group moving forward. Success in achieving the goals as a group binds the boys closer to the members of that group and helps them identify their personal success with the collective success—the group's "greatness" becomes their own.

As we saw earlier, group games are popular with boys both as participants and spectators because the games allow them to individually participate in great feats and heroic actions in ways that they could not do as individuals. Traditional male organizations such as the military, teams, and scouts have successfully leveraged this desire, helping boys and young men find meaning by:

- Setting out a clear pathway to develop their personal skills
- Giving them a place to attain mastery (and ultimately self-mastery)
- Using their developed skills in service to help the group achieve worthy goals—and thus attain greatness together

These types of group activities help boys experience a personal pathway to greatness that comes not by dominating others, but by serving them. Using this powerful approach to help a boy create meaning in relation to his learning at school is the greatest gift a parent or teacher can bestow on him, not to mention everyone who will interact with him in the future!

Meaningful Work

We all know that success in life requires work. But it also requires meaning. In Keen for Learning I referred to the concept of "meaningful work" developed by author Malcolm Gladwell in his book Outliers: The Story of Success. In trying to understand what made people successful, particularly if the odds were against them, he identified meaningful work as that thing into which people were willing to throw their hearts and souls with the hope of getting something back. Meaningful work has three characteristics:

- **Autonomy** – The structure of it allows one to control how to approach a task and make decisions about it without undue constraints.
- **Complexity** – The task is challenging to the mind and requires ongoing adaptation and innovation.
- **Close relationship between effort and reward** – It is clear to the those engaged in the work that if they put their effort into it, they will see progress toward a goal that is deemed worthy in their eyes.

Those engaged in meaningful work have a visible passion for what they are doing and often display incredible amounts of motivated engagement and discretionary effort. Consequently, their odds of success are much greater. Our goal in educating children should be to help them find that meaningful work that will unleash their potential and share it with the world. Alas, for many boys in school, meaningful work may be hard to come by.

Meaning and school

We've seen that meaning for boys is grounded in utility, in what something is "good" for. Early in life, they seek meaning from the physical experiences of watching and manipulating objects, as well as through interaction and feedback with their first teachers—their parents. A great deal of this feedback is given nonverbally with smiles, hugs, and gestures, and both boys and girls become adept at reading adult body language even before they use a lot of words. But because boys' brains wire so strongly to perceive and take pleasure in movement, what they see and physically experience has more meaning for them than words. Girls often begin using language earlier and more frequently because their verbal processing ability is much stronger from an earlier age. Parents can observe this in their young sons' approach to television; often, they make fewer efforts to interact with the characters on-screen than girls, who will frequently "talk back" to the television. By the time they start school, their lack of oral language skills can affect their view of learning in negative ways.

Since boys enter school trusting their experience much more than words, their tendency is to navigate the world by doing rather than talking. It is easy to see how this can translate into "anti-social" school behavior in young boys, which is characterized by inattention to teachers' verbal instructions, impulsive actions, grabbing, hitting, and an inability to sit still; not to mention outbursts of anger and frustration when their attempts to get what they want fail and they can't use words well enough to change that. As a school principal, I saw this frequently in the students I disciplined in the younger grades, 90% of whom were boys with a tremendous kinesthetic orientation and limited verbal skills. By the time I was called to intervene, however, these boys were already developing a sense of disconnect with the classroom; the behaviors they previously used naturally to help them learn with joy and passion were not working as well in school. Without access to those tools to help them find meaning through experience, they found the classroom an alien place–one where fitting in became a daily challenge.

It is important to emphasize that this is not due to any moral failing of the teacher. Most kindergarten and primary school teachers I know love their students and want to give them every opportunity to succeed. That often takes the form of verbal praise and encouragement, telling a struggling boy, "I know you can do this!" This phrase, however, is much less effective with a boy for a number of reasons. Often, he can't believe the words. Just saying it does not convince him unless he can see by experience that indeed he can do it. Indeed, a boy may come to believe that a teacher's words don't contain truth, or worse, that they are the vehicle for untruths and are only useful to avoid unpleasant situations or to manipulate people into doing what you want.

Even more subtle and injurious is the body language dynamic between the student and teacher. This dynamic is something over which the teacher has little control and even less awareness. We know that most of human communication is actually nonverbal, and research has shown that the human face has more than 40 facial muscles that subconsciously telegraph our true feelings even when we try to pretend otherwise. A boy's first teacher is his mother, who usually loves him no matter what he does. That love is communicated in body language, even when things are difficult or frustrating. In essence, this is the role of the mother, and it frees a child to explore the limits of his abilities.

The first teachers a boy has in school are also usually female, but they have a different mandate: to help a child progress in school by demonstrating achievement in the classroom. Since most teachers of the younger grades take their roles exceedingly personally—with their own self-worth tied to being an effective teacher—they can become frustrated with a boy who doesn't "get it" and whose whole approach to learning seems antithetical to how one needs to learn in the classroom. When working with a child who is resistant or unable to complete a simple task the teacher knows he can complete, the words may be *"C'mon, I know you can do it" but the subconscious facial language he reads is "What's wrong with you? Why can't you please me?"* This is devastating to a young boy because he wants to please the teacher and wants her love and admiration, in the same way he needed it from his mother, but everything he does naturally seems to result otherwise. This fate can befall the interaction between parents and boys when their son begins to experience problems at school and their own unconscious body language—which their son is an expert at reading—telegraphs that he is less worthy as a person than he was before the school struggles occurred.

Beyond the words, a boy's physical experience of being habitually redirected, reprimanded, and reminded of the classroom rules gives him the message that he does not really fit in there. Even when, because of his developmental delays, a boy is given more "play time" in kindergarten, while the more verbal girls sit on the carpet and talk with the teacher, he knows that what he's doing is not as useful in the teacher's eyes. Because he senses no real usefulness for his being in the classroom, the classroom setting begins to lose meaning for him. While others seem to obviously be able to succeed and enjoy the challenges, he perceives he cannot. As a consequence, his need for accomplishment and mastery will have to be satisfied elsewhere.

And so begins a predictable pattern of disengagement that often has many characteristics: slower acquisition of skills, lower achievement, less willingness to take up academic challenges, more frequent conflicts with peers, teachers, and school authorities, more absences from class, more experimentation with illegal substances, and a greater likelihood of dropping out of school. Note that most of these behaviors fall into the fight-or-flight category—reactions that rely on the primitive protective mechanism found in the amygdala, which is larger and more quickly accessed in males.

With every year of disengagement, it becomes increasingly more difficult to help these boys succeed in school. As a principal, I observed that sometime around grade 3, boys seem to decide whether school is "their thing," and thereafter their perceptions harden, with those who decided against school showing ever-increasing levels of fight-or-flight behavior. Having completed the research for this book, I now believe that my perceptions were accurate and that the increased levels of testosterone beginning at this age are the triggers for it, driving these little boys with greater intensity to attain significance and greatness in some area, so that their lives make sense to them and have meaning. To do this, they naturally turn to the places that will make learning and understanding natural for them: movement, game, humor, challenge, and mastery.

For a parent of a young boy new to school or preparing to go, my words in the previous paragraphs may seem alarming. They are not intended to scare you, but to alert you. With awareness of your son's potential pitfalls and the importance of him finding meaning in learning at home and school, you can be better prepared to consciously support him.

Using meaning to help boys learn

It is helpful to look again at our target imagery. Note the progression:

HBL Secret Target Tool™

Where boys are easily met

Where males excel

Where they find fulfilment

Boys will automatically display greater levels of engagement when movement, game, and humor are used in conjunction with learning and learning tasks. Weaving them into boys' learning experiences will make things easier for both the learners and the adults who are trying to teach them. Once a boy is engaged, it is important to use challenge and mastery to help bring out the commitment and passion that will help him become a successful learner at school, home, and beyond.

MEANING AT HOME

The ultimate goal is to help boys find *meaning* in learning, and that is where the greatest benefits are realized. When you are trying to make use of the information in this book at home, there are four ways to apply it for success:

1. Give boys a place to fit
2. Leverage teamwork
3. Make what is learned useful
4. Recognize success and its components

Let's look at some ideas for each one:

Giving boys a place to fit

Boys must ultimately answer the existential question "What am I good for?" You can help answer that question so that it involves being good at learning at home and at school. The goal is to help him find meaning as part of a process of "conscious growth," where he will use his all-important discretionary effort to find his place in any learning situation in which he is placed. As with mastery, there are important things you can do at home which will set the stage for success at school. If a boy consciously understands that learning is meaningful and important at home and that he has proved he is "good for learning" there, it will be easier for you as a parent to help him overcome challenges that the school learning may pose. This is particularly important for young boys. When they have meaningful tasks that use movement, game, humor, challenge and mastery to help them learn, they will develop into more passionate learners and better collaborators with their teachers and classmates. Let's look at few ways to do this:

Linking movement to meaning – Have a boy use his natural movement ability to learn something that is useful around the house. For example, you could ask him to figure out and then physically set up the most efficient way to set the table for dinner, rake up leaves in the yard, or organize his toys or video games for easy access. Once he has done this, make sure to point out that he has demonstrated how good he is at taking on a learning challenge. This will help him to experience that learning is natural, feels good and that he is good at it!

If your son clearly loves to move, asking him to physically illustrate anything he is in the process of learning is a useful step in bringing meaning to the learning task. This includes things like:

- Reading a story book
- Journal writing
- Reviewing what was learned today at school
- Doing a homework assignment
- Studying for a test
- Planning a project

Using a KEEN Learning activity like *Still Life* or *Handy Memory* can matter-of-factly let a parent improve a boy's learning and motivation by showing first, explaining next, and then writing last, when full engagement and understanding is achieved.

Another approach is making little YouTube-type videos where a parent videotapes a boy physically and humorously illustrating the concepts and skills used for that evening's homework. We

To see a video sample of these movement for meaning activities, go to helpingboyslearn.com and enter MN1 in the HBL TIP BOX.

know from the brain research that the memory often better retains bizarre or humorous representations and this will make his performance on a test better and more enjoyable! These can then be shared with family, friends, teachers, and classmates.

Gamifying it – We know that game is one of the secrets for engaging boys in learning, but it is also powerful for bringing meaning to their learning experience. As I pointed out earlier, the secret to using games to enhance meaning is to connect them intimately with the learning. It is much less effective to let a boy play a game after he has done his homework than to make it part of the homework. In Chapter 2, we saw how games like Beat the clock, Beat the Boss and Beat the Best could be applied to learning tasks. A very powerful way to attach meaning to these games is to ask a boy who has been successful to explain how he did it as if he is now the expert. The audience can be family, friends, siblings, or other classmates; it is particularly effective if he can explain to other boys. The method of explanation can be in person, writing in email or social media, or creating a short video that is posted for others. This will enhance his language skills, give him recognition as a learner, and may even cause other males to listen to his secrets of success so that they can use them next time!

Another way to bring meaning to learning, particularly with tedious homework tasks, is to have the boy create a game that requires knowing the material to win. Those of us who have been teachers know that sometimes the only time we really understood what our students had to learn came as we tried to figure out how to teach it to them! We also know that it is hard to engage struggling students in the repetition necessary to learn some concepts and skills When they are asked to create and play a series of games that accomplish the same goal, however, they enthusiastically participate. Creating a game can be done instantaneously ("Can you come up with a simple game in five minutes that would test me on what you just learned about fractions?"). After playing it with you, he could challenge another adult, a grandparent, a parent, a sibling, or a friend. Because it brings meaning to the homework, it can take some of the stress out of the process for both parent and child!

Finding a fit with humor – In the chapter on humor, I discussed ways that humor can engage boys in learning because it focuses their attention, reduces their fear of failure, and connects them to others. I also pointed out that boys need to understand the context and situation if they are going to use humor for the best effect. Home is a place where you can allow a boy with an active funny bone to use it more freely, as long as it helps him to complete the learning tasks with more joy. Asking him to think about the silly side of the material by challenging him to:

- make up a joke about it
- draw a cartoon
- come up with a silly poem or limerick
- imagine what would happen if it were learned the wrong way
- think of the most painful way to learn it
- describe what aliens from another planet would think if they had to do it
- create a fake video "news flash" about it

These are all ways to let him apply his sense of humor to what he has to learn. They may not be appropriate for the school context and that's OK. But you may decide to that he needs to abide by the home version of a well-known warning: "**Don't** try this at school!"

Make him the Explainer – We know that young boys who do not get the opportunity to practice speaking tend to struggle more in school. You can help your son fit in better at school as well as improve his language skills by using his desire for challenge and mastery. Ask him to explain things to you and others—things as simple as how to score a goal in soccer, what types of things the family does for holidays, or the reason he has to brush his teeth. Start by saying something like, "Jon, you're good at explaining things. Why are there so many cars outside on the weekend?" As he gives his explanation, prompt him to expand with *who, what, where, when,* and *why* questions. If he doesn't know, he may want to check on the internet. But make it easy and fun—not an "assignment." When he has finished, let him know that you appreciated him explaining that and find other opportunities to let him explain it to others. You will notice that he gets better at it. He will become more confident and often use his mastery impulse to improve, and you'll be happy knowing that his brain is making better neural connections that will serve him well at school!

To see a videoexample with a list of questions for the "Explainer," go to helpingboyslearn.com and enter MN2 in the HBL TIP BOX.

Leveraging teamwork

We have seen that boys will often cooperate better within the context of a team. It shows them where they fit into the whole, allows them to channel their competitive instincts, and provides a pathway to mastery and recognition. This can be very useful for teachers trying to help boys find meaning and there are some very specific approaches that work well (see the Teacher-Tip sheet at the end of the chapter). At home, where there may not be as many others to "team" with, parents can still foster skills that will help a boy find meaning in learning by working with a family and friends.

Within family projects – A bit of thought can help a parent turn a normal family activity (cleaning at home, getting ready for a trip, planning a surprise party) into an opportunity for a boy to see the value of learning with others. Make sure that he knows what the focus of the activity is and then make it clear to him what his part is. Using the 5W's from the mastery chapter can be useful in showing him what his role is in making the effort a success and identifying exactly how he can do that. You can practice school skills by having him make lists, write invitations, make a video journal, or email important information. What is important is that his contribution is recognized—not with a reward—but as a reinforcement of how well he learns and is able to use his skills.

In pairs with siblings/friends – You don't need to wait for a family project to happen to focus on teamwork for learning. Little tasks that he is asked to undertake with a younger sibling can be just as effective. For example, a boy and his sister could be asked to design a better organization plan for toys in the playroom so that everyone enjoys it better. This could involve making a written plan, sharing it with the family, and then making the changes they have suggested. The key to success here is that they both understand that success can only be attained together and that if they both can succeed you will recognize that success.

Making learning useful

When we understand how important utility is for most boys, it is easier to understand why they may say in school, "Why do we have to learn this?" It is not a declaration of laziness, but a request for the teacher to make the learning meaningful. "You're going to need this in high school" is no help to an eight-year-old! He may very well need it, but it is too far away to motivate him in the short term. Parents need to understand this too. Below are a few ways you can support a boy's school success at home by showing him how something he learns can be useful immediately. To do that, game, challenge, and mastery are great secrets to apply! Some examples:

Stand and deliver – Every night ask your son to stand up and give a one to two sentence description of what was learned at school today and why it was important. If they can do it, make sure it's publicly recognized visually with a checklist or token. Make it fun and exciting, and feel free to allow them two minutes' time to plan beforehand.

"What's this good for?" – Take something your son had to learn this week at school and give him a timed, 10-minute window with access to the Internet. Challenge him to figure out how what he is learning could be useful to:

    a. An individual

    b. A group

    c. A country

A small prize/reward can we awarded if they can do it within the time frame.

Teaching others – Inviting a boy to teach someone else what he has learned is tremendously effective in triggering his challenge and mastery needs. It makes the material more useful to him by engaging his need to serve. I have seen this strategy used to great effect when boys are told before learning that they will be asked to teach someone younger than them about the concept afterward. If you know that your son is going to have to prepare for a test, let him teach the material to you, a sibling, or another willing listener.

Recognizing success and its components

Because mastery is a pathway to learning for boys, it is important to bring meaning to it for boys by letting them know and giving them recognition when it has been attained. In conjunction with the strategies emphasized in the mastery chapter, adding the following elements can be useful:

Visually represent the steps to success – A visual map or storyboard of the steps to successful completion of an assignment is very helpful as it situates a boy's progress in a way that connects

To see examples of a visual map and download a template to use with your son, to to helpingboyslearn.com and enter MN3 in the HBL TIP BOX.

to his visual-spatial abilities. If your son comes home with a project and this hasn't already been done, create a visual map with him and post it where everyone can see it. A 5W plan can also be helpful here!

"Describe how you did it..." – When a boy succeeds at a school task, brings home a good mark, or is praised by the teacher for getting an assignment done, take a moment to ask him to explain how and why he was successful and to describe the challenges he had to overcome along the road to achievement. Sharing this description with others (parents, grandparents, friends, classmates) in person or online helps him be conscious of how his own efforts and abilities produce results in school.

Who else helped? – Similar to above, but when he succeeds at a school task, instead of having a boy explain what he did to achieve success, ask him to explain what the other people contributed and identify why it could not have been completed without each of them. For example, a teacher worked to create and mark the assignment; classmates helped him understand what to do; Mom checked it over before he handed it in; his sister turned the TV down so he could work. Reflecting on this helps him realize that he is part of a community of learning that is there to help him and that he has responsibilities as part of that community to be of service in his turn.

Connecting with successful near-aged older males – In my experience, linking boys up with other boys who are between two to four years older in a mentorship relationship has been a very successful way for them to bring meaning to their learning and help them be future-oriented in their approach to learning. Ask the older boys to talk about their younger selves and why it was important for them to learn in earlier years in order to be successful later. Have them describe challenges they faced, how they felt in their successes and failures, and their own dreams for the future. This can set the stage for a discussion with your son about his dreams and goals for the future.

> **For a teacher tip sheet that has strategies for helping boys find meaning in class work, go to helpingboyslearn.com and enter MNT in the HBL TIP BOX.**

AFTERWORD

Preparing Your Son for the 21st Century
Use the 6 secrets to ensure his success

"We may not be able to prepare the future for our children,
but we can at least prepare our children for the future."
—Franklin D. Roosevelt

In a world of rapid change, it is increasingly important that young people be motivated to learn and continue that learning throughout their lives—both alone and in collaboration with others. Only in this way will they reach their full potential and find a meaningful, positive place in society. To do this, "21st century skills" are needed. These skills, identified widely by academic and business groups, are as important as traditional academics. As a parent, these "real-world" skills are no doubt ones that you see demanded everyday in your own work experience:

1. Critical thinking/problem solving
2. Oral/written communication
3. Information technology application
4. Ethics/social responsibility
5. Teamwork/collaboration
6. Diversity

7. Leadership
8. Creativity/innovation
9. Professionalism/work ethic
10. Lifelong learning/self-direction

- (From The Partnership for 21st Century Skills, www.p21.org)

The majority of these are "soft skills," requiring both skill and character development. Schools are being asked to develop these skills, but if we want boys to be successful, we know how influential parents and guardians can be. The six secrets in this book can be used as tools to help boys learn and achieve best both at home and in the classroom, but their value is deeper than that.

Positive male character development and acquisition of 21st century skills require that males re-channel many of their natural ways of learning in new ways. Fifty years ago, there were a myriad of social organizations (Boy Scouts, community sports teams, and religious youth groups, for example) that actively encouraged the positive channeling of movement, game, and humor for the challenge and mastery necessary to encourage males to find meaning by making themselves of service to society. They stood apart from schools as alternate sources of learning and supported families, particularly in the area of character development. Today those organizations have decreasing influence in the lives of many boys, and many families are fractured, overburdened, and still in need of support in this area. And the six pathways to learning are still "secrets" because, while some teachers and parents have used them intermittently in the past, they have not been used consciously, purposefully, or on a wide scale to help boys learn in school.

For ongoing tips to help your son with these all-important 21st century skills, go to helpingboyslearn.com and enter NEWSLETTER in the HBL TIP BOX.

Know what your son needs

The most powerful question you can ask yourself about your son's education is: "What does he need to be a successful learner?" Understanding that boys and girls learn differently makes the response to this question much more effective. Figure 6 summarizes some of the gender differences that affect boys and girls as they learn in a school setting.

Area	Boys	Girls
Movement & Visual-Spatial Awareness	More neural wiring in right side of brain to perceive/appreciate movement. Male brains are more active with physical/visual movement	Less wiring and less perception/appreciation of objects moving in space
Language	Develops later because it is processed only on left side of brain. Words often used thoughtlessly because they don't mean as much as actions	Easier oral self-expression due to processing of neural wiring for language on both sides of brain
Working With Others	Will participate if it helps them win or achieve personal or group goal	Will participate to build social capital and harmony
Conflict	Clarifies relationships	Ruptures relationships
Competition	Causes increased focus; sincere desire to win	Can cause anxiety if social structure threatened
Neurochemicals	Testosterone predominant; released in competition and "winning"	Oxytocin predominant; released when girls "tend and befriend," creating social harmony
Information/ Learning	Valued for utility	Valued for social integration
Hearing	Not as well developed; appreciation for loud noises	Acute; sensitivity to teachers who speak too loud
Homework	Do less at every level	Usually put more effort into it
Relationship With Teacher	Not important by itself; relevant if it increases sense of significance	Important to help identify classroom social structure and her place within it
Timed Tasks	Increases focus, productivity	Increases anxiety, reduces productivity
Emotions	Processed in primitive amygdala	Processed in frontal lobes
Physical Pain	Skin less sensitive	Skin more sensitive

These differences are important if we want boys to excel in the applied "soft skills" in school. Yet, as we noted at the beginning of the book, many are becoming increasingly disengaged from learning and school, succeeding less often than girls, and pursuing higher education less frequently. It is their inability to learn the applied skills necessary for success in our modern world and their disengagement from learning in formal environments that threaten to become lifelong handicaps, tragically affecting themselves and society. Unless we are able to motivate more boys to learn and succeed in school, they will become unable to participate productively in the economy and society of the future. In response to this stress, they may move increasingly toward the two extremes that their physiology and evolutionary tendencies have hard-wired into them. On one hand, they will trigger the "fight" response, seeking to gain testosterone-fuelled personal triumphs over others while becoming increasingly alienated, potentially violent, and susceptible to demagogues and anti-social behavior. Alternately, they will take "flight" into immaturity, video games, and online fantasy, remaining immature, useless children who expect the women in their lives to carry them. The information you now have can be an important antidote to either of these outcomes.

CONCLUSION

Coming to the end of this book, I hope that you feel that the knowledge you have gained about how boys learn will help you improve the success of the boys in your life. I hope that the six "secrets" described in this book give you a better idea of things you can do to help those boys learn and thrive. These "secrets" are user-friendly to parents and teachers. Anyone can use them immediately. Once you start seeing a boy's behavior through the lens of movement, game, humor, challenge, mastery, and meaning, you will find yourself better able to help him engage passionately and effectively in learning.

Finally, I hope this book is the beginning of a conversation. The ideas and strategies suggested here are only a few of those that can be used in this framework. For more, I invite you to become part of our community on Facebook and at www.helpingboyslearn.com. By sharing our struggles and successes, we can and do help others to do the same. Then these six important pathways to boys' learning will be "secrets" no more. Rather, they will form the basis for helping our boys grow into the kind of men we know they can be.

FURTHER READING

Dixon, E. J. (2010). *KEEN for Learning: Why some students don't succeed in the classroom and what we can do about it.* Barrie, Ontario, Canada: Wintertickle Press

Gladwell, M., (2008). *Outliers: The Story of Success.* New York, NY: Penguin.

Gurian, M., Stevens, K., & King, K. (2008). *Strategies for teaching boys and girls – elementary level: A workbook for educators.* San Francisco, CA: Jossey-Bass.

Gurian, M. (2011). *Boys and Girls Learn Differently! A Guide for Teachers and Parents.* San Francisco, CA: Jossey-Bass

Sax, L. (2006). *Why gender matters: What parents and teachers need to know about the emerging science of sex differences.* New York, NY: Three Rivers Press.

Sax, L. (2007). *Boys adrift: The five factors driving the growing epidemic of unmotivated boys and underachieving young men.* New York, NY: Basic Books.

Brown, S. L., & Vaughan, C. (2009). *Play: How it shapes the brain, opens the imagination, and invigorates the soul.* New York, NY: Avery.

Newkirk, T. (2002). *Misreading masculinity: Boys, literacy, and popular culture* (pp. 126-128). Portsmouth, NH: Heinemann.

Wilhelm, J. D., & Smith, M. (2002). *"Reading don't fix no Chevys": Literacy in the lives of young men.* Portsmouth, NH: Heinemann.

For an updated list of other books and resources to deepen your understanding of boy's learning, go to helpingboyslearn.com and enter READ in the HBL TIP BOX.

HELPING BOYS LEARN
6 Secret Strategy List